Insights that educators, students, parents, coaches, and employers may want to consider.

How do we support meaningful learning?

- Take Risks
- Don't Fix Anything
- Take Emotions Into Consideration
- Make Students Feel Smart and Safe
- Take Past Experiences Into Consideration
- Join the Art of Teaching with the Science of Learning

Modernizing Approaches to Learning is a must read resource about the brain's connection to the nature of learning that joins the art of teaching with the science of learning.

Hebron, a PGA Hall of Fame member, compiled studies from several fields of science which support learning faster while retaining skills and information longer.

Filled with counterintuitive insights and non-traditional suggestions that enhance approaches for learning anything. Any provider or receiver of information will find this book a useful read.

Scan to hear Michael
speak about this book.

Modernizing Approaches to Learning

Exchanging 20th Century Teaching for 21st Century Learning

By Michael Hebron

Title page

Modernizing Approaches to Learning

Exchanging 20th Century Teaching for 21st Century Learning
First Edition - published in 2013 by
Learning Golf, Inc.
495 Landing Avenue, Smithtown NY 11787
(http://www.michaelhebron.com) and
(http://www.nlglive.com) aka Neuro Learning for Golf Live
Copyright 2013 Michael Hebron
ISBN: 978-1-937069-05-6

Printed in the United States of America by LightningSource, Inc.
This book is Sustainable Forestry Initiative® (SFI®) certified.
(www.lightningsource.com)

Editorial assistance by Nannette Poillon McCoy

Cover Design by April Scarduzio

Library of Congress Cataloging-In-Publishing Data

Hebron, Michael

Modernizing Approaches to Learning/Michael Hebron, 1st ed.

Includes bibliography references

Library of Congress Control Number   201393540

Preamble

In the 21st century it's unacceptable for students not to make progress at a reasonable rate when instructors and students could benefit from what science has uncovered about learning. *Modernizing Approaches to Learning* discusses research related to the brain as the gateway to learning. When taking a brain-compatible approach to learning, we can learn faster and retain information and skills longer.

The author discusses findings from neuroscience, cognitive science, physiological and psychological research about the brain and learning. He offers practical, modern ways to move from damaging educational approaches toward emotionally safe, self-discovery and self-reliant approaches. Approaches that are geared to help are not as valuable as those geared for self-help. Modernized approaches join the art of teaching with the science of learning (which is where research demonstrates that we learn naturally through trial and error adjustments).

To educate, means "to lead out from." The task is to lead learning out of student's minds that are filled with memories of wanted and unwanted outcomes, not to impose it. Many learning approaches stop too early and do not utilize brain-compatible learning approaches that encourage students to use their past experiences and unconscious minds.

How words are used tops the list of elements that create learning conducive environments. Learners subjected to criticism, or suggestion that they were unsuccessful, do not respond as well as those who receive positive encouragement to experiment further.

Another insight in this book that merits serious attention is that approaches to learning that attempt to fix unwanted outcomes are not as useful as approaches that enhance a student's learning potential. The author suggests avoiding a get-it-right approach (trying to get to a performance level by following someone else's path to a solution).Instead, utilize a learn-and-develop approach – to arrive at a performance or solution based on personal trial and error adjustments and recognize that a personal target or solution was met.

"My gift of fantasy has meant more to me than my talent for absorbing knowledge." Albert Einstein

Good brains, Poor learning

Everyone who comes into the world with a healthy brain is predisposed to be a competent natural learner. Learning is a survival skill that we are all born with. Why then does poor learning exist? How can the brain, the most efficient learning machine we know of, take part in poor learning?

The building blocks for learning, developing, and performing up to one's potential are found in a brain compatible approach to learning. The best way to learn is to have some understanding of what suppresses and what supports the nature of meaningful learning. When using words and thoughts that are not emotionally compatible with the brain's connection to learning some approaches to learning become dehumanizing.

"Peace of mind" can be the most important emotional tool for optimizing acts of learning. When the approach to learning makes people feel smart and safe, it creates the kind of mind set that supports reaching one's potential. Modernized 21st century approaches to learning develop skills that are able to develop more skills.

Keep in mind that scientists have reported significant gains in student performance through game based approaches to learning new information. When encoded in a game-like environment, knowledge that is useful under present conditions becomes useful under different conditions as well.

About the Author

Michael Hebron has received over twenty-five awards, including the national teacher of year. Michael has been invited to speak at Yale, MIT, in India, Australia, Canada, Finland, Chile, Japan, Costa Rica, England, Ireland, France, Italy, Wales, Switzerland, Czech Republic, Spain, and as a private and public speaker to organizations, businesses, universities and school districts throughout the United States. Michael has authored five books and over one hundred articles; has been a guest on several TV shows including the Charlie Rose Show and NBC's Today Show; has taken numerous classes at Harvard's Graduate School of Education Connecting the Mind-Brain to Education Institute. Michael would say he has been researching the brain's connection to learning with lots of help from award-winning educators and scientists for over two decades. What happens after a lesson is his concern.

He provides continuing education scholarships at three high schools in New York (the High School of Public Service in Brooklyn; Holy Cross High School in Queens; and Smithtown High School on Long Island, NY).

It has been said that Michael has the curiosity of a child; the soul of a poet; and the heart of a fighter, all wrapped up in years of experience. He has been referred to as the Teacher of Teachers who shares counter-intuitive insights and promotes non-traditional ideas to think about. In 2013 Michael had the honor of being indoctrinated into the PGA of America Hall of Fame.

Some of the associations in which Michael Hebron holds membership include:

Learning and the Brain Society (LBS)

American Society of Training and Development (ASTD)

American College of Sports Medicine (ACSM)

National Center for Science Education (NCSE)

Association for Scholastic Curriculum Development (ASCD)

Phi Delta Kappa International Education Association (PDKIEA)

High School Coaches Association (HSCA)

Professional Golf Association of America (PGA)

United States Golf Association (USGA)

"When one decides to take learning seriously enough to do it as efficiently and enjoyably as possible, then one must take the brain's connection to learning seriously."

George Elliott - 1860

http://www.michaelhebron.com

Acknowledgements

Not a day passes without my appreciation for the large number of resources that have directly and indirectly influenced what I have compiled here. That this book bears only one author's name is unfair. I thank everyone who has helped me gain new insights about the nature of learning that I did not have during the first twenty years I was teaching. For the most part, I am sharing what I have learned from others about the brain's connection to learning.

A special thanks to the staff at Harvard University's Connecting the Mind-Brain to Education Institute (where I have taken classes) and its director Kurt Fischer. I also want to thank Eric Jensen, who organized several seminars about the brain's connection to learning that I attended. This book is a progress report on how my insights about learning and teaching have changed over time. The tone of the book was influenced by suggestions and questions from Ryan Hayden, Nicholas Renna, Nannette Poillon McCoy, Professor Stephen Yazulla. (NY University at Stony Brook), Susan Berdoy Meyers, and every individual I have had the opportunity to help learn more efficiently.

In the mid-1960s Gene Borek, a man I had the highest respect for, suggested that I should write down my impressions of what I was reading, studying, and experiencing. Gene suggested I write on a scheduled basis - daily, weekly, or monthly, the choice was mine to make as long as I wrote. He felt that if I had a personal record of my thoughts and impressions I would be able to look back and learn from my journey of development. Because of Gene Borek, who passed on in 2011, I have been making notes on a daily basis for over four decades. Thank you Gene Borek, you are missed.

Everyone in modern science who has been researching the brain's connection to learning has a big thank-you from me. Because of these men and women we now have a modern model

VI

that enhances approaches to learning without having to know every aspect of how brains operate. Without being a cognitive scientist choices can now be made that design brain-compatible approaches to learning. Over 130 universities around the world are involved in what is called the "Human Brain Project" in an effort to expand insights about the brain. I thank all of them!

What science has uncovered about the brain's connection to learning will be added to and adjusted by more research in the future. But what has already been put forward by leading scientists and educators about the topic of meaningful learning has made a huge positive impact in a variety of learning environments. Individuals are now learning faster and retaining information and skills longer than in the past.

It has been said that any provider of information should not tell their audience that they are wrong – that would be a NO-NO! It has also been said that one can rarely, if ever, help someone who has not asked for help. We cannot force new ideas on someone who is not curiously open. Curiosity may be the most useful way of looking at motivation and the nature of learning.

Based on knowledge of what studies suggest should be re-thought about approaches to learning, I respectfully suggest the following: **It would be a huge oversight not to approach learning and teaching without some understanding of the brain's connection to the process of change.**

This suggestion is true for both providers and receivers of information. Learning and teaching "with the brain in mind"[1] supports reaching one's potential. Knowing both the power and the limitations of the approach to learning that is being used can help individuals avoid damaging conflicts that can arise during acts of learning without these insights.

[1] Eric Jensen

Contents

Foreword

See this book as a conversation about the rapidly changing views on approaches to learning that are being driven by the curiosity of respected research.

The brain is our gateway to learning. Leveraging the brain's connection to that process of change is one of the topics of this book.

Everyone believes that learning is a good thing, but most of us know so little about how it actually takes place. Some approaches to learning try to accomplish external outcomes without taking into consideration how the brain internally process, decodes, encodes and recalls information.

The bookends of growth and development are the brain on one side; the nature of learning on the other side; with meaningful learning in the middle. The more we know about the brain's connection to learning, the more prepared we are for supporting and experiencing meaningful learning.

Normally, after we gain insights into how something operates, anything can be improved, including acts of learning. The aim: use "Grow the Brain" instruction by combining the Art of Teaching with the Science of Learning and exchange 20th century teaching for 21st century learning. Unfortunately, some elements of the nature of learning are non-traditional and counterintuitive, causing them to be undervalued in the past. This book offers non-traditional ideas for some traditional problems by paying attention to the brain's connection to learning.

Peace of mind can be an important emotional tool for optimizing what can support or prevent opportunities to experience meaningful learning.

Non-Conscious

The brain operates and learns by making predictions influenced by information gained from all the differences found in prior outcomes encoded in the non-conscious mind. Random, spontaneous, improvisational thoughts and actions share a common element, RESULTS. These results are all different, creating a variety of useful non-conscious reference points that become the tools of predictions for future use (if this then that). This kind of spontaneous and improvisational learning can support reaching one's personal potential.

Systematic approaches to learning often cause individuals to fear failing to meet the needs of a system. This fear of failure causes an emotional roadblock to the uniquely individual personal process that enables individuals invent skills and gain knowledge.

Yes, there is an alphabet and there are the accepted rules of grammar, but rules cannot tell you what to think or how to create what you personally want to do, or say. Systems and rules have limits when it comes to creativity.

Ultimately the only information and skills that help one to experience meaningful long-term learning are those invented or experienced personally. What does it look like to you? What does it feel like to you? What do you think about it?

When it comes to learning, the influence of the unseen raw material already stored in an unconscious mind is similar to an off-duty supervisors having influence over what happens at work even though they are not present. There really is no new learning. What we already know and have stored in our non-conscious mind has influence over what can be learned, similar to the unseen supervisor's power to influence.

When You Talk About Approaches to Learning You're Forced to Talk About the Brain.

"The brain is the primary organ for learning."

Kurt Fischer

Director of Harvard University's Connecting Mind-Brain to Education Institute

The First Principal for Modernizing Learning:

Pay attention to emotions;

the student's past

experiences;

and the use of language.

"The most powerful drug known to mankind is language."
Rudyard Kipling

- The future of learning lies in the study of the brain, it will untangle the mysteries of how people learn." Dr. Donald Thomas
- "Education makes for better minds and knowledge of the mind makes better education." Daniel T. Willingham
- "An understanding of how the brain learns can influence the design of more effective learning." Center for Educational Research and Innovation
- "What has been uncovered about the brain requires a fundamental change in education." Professor Harry Chugani
- "It is time to become familiar with the latest research on learning; it's a positive message for all of us." Renate Caine, Professor of Education at California State University
- "Research into the nature of learning could be summarized by saying; typical educators and popular instruction approaches routinely violate what modern science now knows about how most people learn efficiently." *How People Learn,* by John D. Bransford

Why is the human brain wired to operate and learn the way it does? Because for millions of years when our ancestors were surviving and thriving, that is how the brain wired itself to operate. "The human mind is a product of evolution." [2]

Homo Sapiens <u>means</u> Smart Beings

"Your brain is involved in everything you do, including how you think, how you feel, and how you act."
Dr. Joe Dispenza

---

[2] *How the Mind Works,* Stephen Pinker, p. 40

A Mission Statement for Learning

- **HONOR EACH INDIVIDUAL AND THEIR CHOICES**
- **PROMOTE SELF-RELIANCE**
- **STRIVE FOR PERSONAL GROWTH**
- **SUPPORT SELF-UNDERSTANDING AND SELF-ESTEEM**
- **ENCOURAGE CURIOSITY AND IMAGINATION**
- **ENHANCE WHAT ALREADY WORKS**
- **PROVIDE A POSITIVE EMOTIONAL ENVIRONMENT**
- **AVOID NEGATIVE JUDGMENTS AND CORRECTIONS**
- **HELP STUDENTS FEEL SMART**
- **IMPROVE OBSERVATION SKILLS AND SEEING OPTIONS**
- **SUPPORT SELF-DEVELOPMENT, SELF-ORGANIZATION, SELF-DISCOVERY, SELF-ASSESSMENT**
- **UNCOVER ORDINARY THINGS THAT PRODUCE EX-TRAORDINARY RESULTS**
- **WORK WITH BROAD CONCEPTS; THE GIST OF THINGS**

One goal of a modernized, brain-compatible approach to learning is to make approaches for learning less frustrating and more enjoyable. Students in S.M.A.R.T ™, S.A.F.E. ™, P.L.A.Y.F.U.L™ learning environments will move forward, evaluating the experience after it happens. On the other hand, in unsafe teach-to-fix-to get-it-right environments, students have concerns before they act. Modernized approaches to learning motivate individuals toward higher-order thinking in emotionally safe conditions that are conducive to producing unforgettable learning.

SMART = **S**tudents' **M**inds **A**re **R**eally **T**alented (No one is broken or in need of fixing)

SAFE = **S**tudents **A**lways **F**irst **E**nvironments (Emotionally and physically safe environments)

PLAYFUL = **P**owerful **L**earning **A**bout **Y**ourself **F**inds **U**seful **L**earning (Supports self-reliance)

Efficient approaches to learning see every individual as a light that is burning bright and they are just helping these students learn to teach themselves to burn even brighter.

Going From Not Knowing to Knowing?

"The starting point of learning is a query, a puzzle that a learner wishes to solve."[3] Many individuals may be looking for insights for solving the following puzzle: When it comes to learning there is an unfortunate and almost scandalous statistic; there are more individuals going to schools and colleges, taking sports instruction, attending business seminars and in other learning environments *who are not reaching their potential than do*! Why?

Being a teacher, I became curious about why people do not reach their potential when learning. In the late 1980s I began to gather research for improving approaches to learning. I started by asking myself two questions; *how* does learning happen and *why* does learning happen? I was looking for some insight into the essential processes that underline learning and developing.

What would I be learning? What blind spots did I have about learning? What part of learning and developing did I overlook? What causes learning and developing delays? Is anyone or anything at fault? What should change? What should we know about the nature of change at the intersection of before, during and after acts of learning?

Discussing acts of learning is always a thorny issue, but the reality is that the approach to learning is either brain-compatible or not, and when it is not, it is less efficient than it could be! *Modernizing Approaches to Learning* is a discussion about the brain's connection to this process of change. For some, what has been complied here may be a different or new way of looking at

---

[3] *The Art and Science of Teaching*, p. 87.

the nature of learning, so keep an open mind. The value of unwanted outcomes and the importance of our emotions to the process of learning and human developing are also being discussed here. The mind-brain connection to learning is experienced every-day and often is not recognized for its value. **Insights that reveal brain-compatible approaches to learning are far more straight-forward than one may believe.**

These insights were not discovered by me, I am only writing about some new and eye-opening research that is at odds with some long held views. These insights from several fields of science have changed both my personal and professional lives. What I have compiled in this book is a modest and cautions effort on my part to share research that supports reaching one's potential. What is behind learning that lasts? Brain-compatible approaches that are sustainable is the view that is being put forward here. Hopefully, both the lay person (not trained in cognitive science) and perhaps some educators and scientists will find this information about the brain's connection to learning useful.

Modernizing

"We are at the beginning of a neuro-scientific revolution and on the threshold of knowing how we know."
Nobel Lauriat Gerald M. Edleman

Modernized approaches to learning have a culture that supports the idea that learning is a transformative adjustment, with accomplishments arriving as if they were always there waiting to be uncovered and drawn out from the indirect preparations that past experiences provided. Twenty years ago I heard two outstanding teachers (Lynn Marriott and Pia Nilsson) refer to this process as out-struction, to which I added, "it is not instruction; it is out-struction!" A modernized approach to learning (out-struction) has a culture that promotes:

- Prevention, not fixing the old way
- Developing strengths, not fixing the old way
- Emotional health, not fixing the old way

Meaningful learning has an origin of internal chemistry that fosters the energy of positive learning when poor outcomes are recognized as important feedback for future reference and not as failure.

The choices that lead to meaningful learning are more about supporting and developing a student's thinking and deduction tools for operating in ever-changing real world environments, than about knowing information. In the long run, "it is looking for solutions that develops flexible knowledge and portable skills,"[4] that support one's natural ability to learn.

The collective aim of experiencing meaningful learning has less of an emphasis on the ability to know information and is more about developing approaches to learning that are using a broad-based framework wrapped in the kind of curiosity that supports motivation – "what's on the next page;" "what can I do next?"

There is often something missing in authority-driven approaches to learning and teaching. As I write this, American students rank only 25th in the world in math and 17th in science. Many of the leading athletes in the world are no longer Americans. When it comes to learning and teaching any skill or subject, are we doing enough to gain more accurate insights about the nature of learning, or are we just gathering more and more details about subject content information.

---

[4] David Wellingham

Myths and Facts

What science has uncovered about the brain's connection to learning will be added to and adjusted by more research in the future. But what has already been presented by leading scientists and educators about the topic of meaningful learning has made a huge positive impact in a variety of learning environments. Individuals are now learning faster and retaining information and skills longer than in the past. Several myths about learning that have been discussed by Harvard's Ellen Langer and others include:

- Myth: Basics should be learned so well that they become second nature
  Fact: Over learning basics at the start can stifle creativity and individual expression

- Myth: Delaying gratification is important
  Fact: Keeping on-going interest and joy in learning leads to more meaningful learning

- Myth: There is a right and wrong way or answer
  Fact: Correctness depends on context

- Myth: Intelligence is knowing what is out there
  Fact: Lifelong learners are not know-it-alls

- Myth: Forgetting is a problem
  Fact: Memory can prevent the formation of new or novel use and application beyond personal biases

- Myth: Memorization is necessary
  Fact: When possible, relating information to personal experiences is better than memorization

- Myth: There is a limit on what can be learned
  Fact: There appears to be no limit to storing information,

unfortunately our ability to recall is limited. Therefore approaches to learning must take care that they support the recall of information

- Myth: Orderly, simple learning is the aim
  Fact: "Students need unpredictable environments in order to gain understanding, thereby creating access to it for the long term. Order does not establish memories that last."
  Robert Bjork UCLA Learning and Forgetting Lab

Modernized approaches for learning are exchanging a teacher-centered, teach-to-fix to get something right approach, for a student-centered, learn-and-develop culture.

In this culture the mind-brain is no longer filled with corrections, nor the fear of failure or other negative emotions when individuals are learning to produce workable outcomes (fear is the most powerful emotion[5]). With this methodology both the provider and the receiver of information experience improved skill development. Educators become more effective and students learn more efficiently with this approach. **In this culture learning involves coaching and teaching to our strengths and is not trying to fix poor outcomes**. There are no nags, demands or yells for students to do better. This methodology is not really new, but has been overlooked by some parents, employers, instructors, coaches, and educators.

Dictionaries define the term modernization as, "Accommodations involving new techniques." Based on the mind-brain connection to learning there are new techniques for learning anything. Today it is possible to be more informed about the nature of learning than ever before.

"Man will occasionally stumble over truth, but usually will manage to walk over or around it, and carry on."
Winston Churchill

---

[5] *The Brain*, by Alexander Blade, p. 88

One hypothesis being put forward here is: when earning a good education, individuals have been guided in the direction of using an approach that develops skills that develop more skills.

"The end of the journey isn't knowing more, it is doing more."
Julie Dirksen author of *For How People Learn*

That said, neuroscientist David Souso pointed out, **"The more teachers (and students) know about how the brain learns (processing information) the more successful they can be."**

There are no magical answers that can make approaches to learning efficient all the time. The *end* is always to create an environment where individuals can *earn* the kind of sense-making skills that birth flexible knowledge and portable skills for use in the ever changing environments of the real world.

Learn-and-develop approaches build on past experiences and what has come before. On the other hand, teach-to-fix to get something right approaches to learning overvalue new information. Fixing isn't learning.

When learning is not moving forward at an acceptable pace there are issues. For members of the human race, having the ability to learn is not one of the issues, but the culture of the approach to learning that is being used can be. You could say that all human beings start out at the head of the class and then, unfortunately, some are caused to fall a distance behind.

Influenced by the nature of learning and the ability to adapt, we are all descendants of the world's first life forms. Today our intelligent human race often finds itself in a predicament when it is not in a learning compatible environment.

The most useful possibilities for applying what is being uncovered about the value of natural learning are found in the brain's connection to learning.

Dr. Haim Ginott, once a member of the White House Committee on Education, a leader in teacher education and Fellow of the

American Psychological Association, said as far back as the 1970s, *"Many teaching problems will be solved in the next few decades. There will be new learning environments and new means of instruction."*

No Support

When is information not supporting meaningful learning? Perhaps a common response would be "when information is false." But many false ideas and poor answers have been the starting point for ground-breaking discoveries.

Information does not fully support learning when:

- It has no meaning to students
- It makes no sense to students
- It cannot be related to a past experience
- It has too many details
- It causes frustration
- It is not developmentally appropriate
- It is not transferable to multiple contexts
- It creates more stress than curiosity
- It is outcome, not process orientated
- It is out of context
- It creates barriers to learning
- It is geared to a learning style
- It is presented only one way
- It is not part of a story or metaphor
- It does not promote self-discovery
- It does not support self-confidence
- It does not improve self-doubt

Slow to Learn

During the first two decades I was teaching I was slow to learn that the student is the real educator, providing information for both themselves and their instructor. I was just giving out information – I was being influenced by a teaching culture that was not helping individuals find or invent their own knowledge base. Perhaps some readers will identify with the following;

I Was:

- Slow to learn that having preconceived ideas about students or having an answer for them can be damaging
- Subject content rich – I was not oriented to the process of learning
- In charge – I was not a collaborator
- Giving answers – I overlooked the value of self-discovery and more importantly what students already know
- Pointing out poor habits and failures – I did not recognize that there is no failure, only usable feedback for future reference (both conscious and non-conscious reference)
- Trying to fix unwanted outcomes – I was not helping to change poor insights
- Reacting to poor outcomes – I was not providing a pro-active learning experience. Some teachers give tests back until the student gets an A
- Trying to teach a subject – I was not supporting a journey of self-learning
- Trying to teach details using expert models – I was not using a learning model consisting of general, non-specific, just in the ball park concepts

- Giving commands – I was not providing guidelines and choices
- Slow to realize that a lesson is an opportunity to experiment, not a time to try to get-it-right
- Trying to improve performance – I was not helping to enhance learning potential

It seems fair to say that students will not reach their potential until providers of information reach their potential. Modernized contemporary approaches to learning take on new meaning when brain-compatible resources are used to reach our goals. Again keep in mind that results are founded on approaches.

It has been said that ignorance is bliss and that what we don't know can't hurt us. When it comes to the approach being used to share information what educators, parents, sports coaches, employers, or any other provider of information do not know about learning can interfere with making progress.

- How do lessons provided become lessons learned?
- Is unforgettable learning available or even possible?
- What influences the brain's ability to take in meaningful information?

As George Elliot said, "The strongest principle of growth lies in human choice. Most everything begins with a belief, or personal insight and choice." What are your beliefs about the topic of learning? Educators, parents, employers and coaches should see themselves as missionaries for learning and not teachers of information while exchanging 20th century teaching for 21st century learning. Daniel T. Willingham (Univ. of Virginia) states, "When learning, individuals do not need evaluators, they need 'missionaries for learning'."

My intention is that any message that is taken from what has been compiled here about learning is timely and timeless. In the past, some approaches to learning that should have been gifts that would keep on giving, were not. There have been times when the nature of learning has been torn apart in some unimaginable ways, moving away from maximizing the potentials of students, employees, and players of sports.

Approaches to learning should not be seen as a grand pursuit, but as supporting a natural arrival of outcomes to be learned from. In the hands of the nature of learning individuals are guided through some misconceptions founded in long held traditional views about learning and the lack of progress they are often responsible for.

Experiencing meaningful learning should not be a long shot gamble, but an opportunity to come to a real time conclusion that reveals the personal potential of all students, with all topics. Today, in the 21st century, any questions about learning and teaching can be rethought with the support of respected research.

Question: Who am I?
I am a survivor
I am the ultimate learner
I am wired for success
Answer: I am the brain in every student!

The brain's connection to learning provides a winning formula; "stick with it" is the message.

Perhaps a closed mind would view what has been compiled here about enhancing approaches to learning as criticism of their approach to learning. But, my only aim is to share insights that I was not aware of, or which were not readily available in the past. After I became curious about the topic of learning I found some interesting studies about the neuro-basics of learning and cognitive development that I have included here. Please enjoy the read.

The nature of learning is filled with ambition, as it should be. It has a long history to be proud of; there are many centuries of meaningful learning in the record books. Over time, the nature of learning was constantly expanding and becoming more advanced as simple one cell development evolved into more complex learning skills.

The nature of learning and (we could say) the nature of man moved on from just adapting and changing, to developing skills that today include complex thinking that is influenced along the way by emotions. Meaningful learning can appear as if learning was not being transferred when its magical nature takes advantage of what looks to be just playful experimentation. Modern approaches to learning have moved beyond the narrow culture of just reacting to unwanted outcomes and the self-deception they cause. In the nature of learning, any discrepancies between wants and outcomes underscore the value of struggle when learning. The nature of learning reaches for the head and the heart, the cognitive and the emotional, and the thinking and feeling mind.

Is a qualified educator someone who knows subject topic information, or someone who understands the nature of learning and the brain's connection to that process? I believe the answer is self-evident: it should be a combination of both. Neurologist Judy Wills, author of *Research Based Strategies to Ignite Student Learning*, wrote, "The past two decades have provided extraordinary progress in our understanding of the nature of learning. We can now see what happens to the brain activity and its structure when students learn. Educators can now relate brain research to helping students learn more effectively and more fully."

As you read on, do so from the perspective that workable learning environments are not focused on changing unwanted outcomes, poor habits, poor grades or poor performances. Efficient approaches to learning are geared more for changing poor insights and improving the learning potential of students so people can learn to change their own unwanted outcomes. Most individuals have the time, talent and resources to make progress and often it is poor insights about learning that fragments their learning potential.

Perhaps the most useful questions a learner should ask are: "How did I come to know what I already know?" "Where would be the best place to start?" "What would be the most natural and efficient approach to learning?" Accurate answers to these kinds of questions would be more valuable for making progress than trying to fix unwanted outcomes.

Brain-compatible learning is about what can be accomplished and not about overcoming some uncertainties. Brain-compatible learning environments are more about what we can do with what has been learned, and what can be said about it, than the details of what something is.

Most individuals probably know more about operating a car than they do about the mind-brain's connection to learning. While it's useful and important to become aware of accurate information or efficient motion patterns, it is also important for individuals to use an approach for learning that is compatible with the way the brain best learns.

> **Approaches that are geared for helping you are not as valuable as modernized approaches that are geared for helping you help yourself.**

"To know that we do not know, what we do not know, that is true knowledge." Copernicus

"Our brain is constantly reorganizing our ideas and experiences; we are the source of our own learning. Our brain organizes sensory data into experiences and then experiences into information."[6]

What follows supports the development of insights to differentiate between:

- Learning approaches vs. teaching approaches
- Learner centered vs. teaching centered
- Process goals vs. outcome goals
- Internal motivation vs. external motivation
- Self-discovery vs. following directions
- Self-evaluation vs. judgments from others
- Non-conscious learning vs. conscious learning

---

[6] P. 26

- Random learning vs. block training
- Learning models vs. expert models
- Feedback vs. failure
- Functional vs. perfection
- Brain-compatible vs. non-brain-compatible

The Brain and
Our Twenty Six Letters

<u>A</u>ctive <u>B</u>rains

<u>C</u>an <u>D</u>evelop <u>E</u>xtraordinary

<u>F</u>uture <u>G</u>rowth;

<u>H</u>ave <u>I</u>nternal <u>J</u>ourneys;

<u>K</u>eep <u>L</u>earning's <u>M</u>eaningful,

<u>N</u>ever-ending <u>O</u>ptions <u>P</u>ossible;

<u>Q</u>uietly <u>R</u>eveal <u>S</u>ights <u>T</u>hat

<u>U</u>ncover <u>V</u>aluable, <u>W</u>orkable,

<u>X</u>-<u>F</u>actors, <u>Y</u>ielding <u>Z</u>est!

Twenty-Six Words About Learning

- Often there is a big misconnect between what many believe about learning and teaching and what modern science has studied and uncovered since the early 1990s.

- Put attention on improving a student's learning potential first. Use brain-compatible approaches in safe classrooms; encourage playful improvement of performance potential to improve learning potential.

- Yes, when it comes to meaningful learning, learning to think; to reason; to improve deduction skills; to learn efficiently, all take precedent over just gathering information.

- When an individual's brain is allowed to do what it has wired itself to do, the nature of learning becomes a natural source of ongoing insights.

- Learning-developing environments are always alive with possibilities, not answers. Information and details are what the culture of teaching and fixing offer, not learning to learn efficiently.

- Any insights about the topic of learning should travel beyond the content to be learned and into the silent language of the process of non-conscious learning.

- Brain-compatible approaches to learning combine the brain's connection to learning and subject content with minds that explore, that question, and that invent – efficiently putting knowledge to use.

- The human brain is a bio-chemical, emotional organ with fascinating capabilities that support the creative process of learning that all human beings can put to use.

- Accept the implications and findings the mind-brain connection to learning provides; they are guidelines enhancing approaches to learning for both providers and receivers of information.

- The act of learning and the brain functions will be heavily influenced by stress; emotions; past experiences; and the environments where our interactions are taking place.

- When individuals cannot use their natural ability to learn, that is a big loss not only to themselves, but also to environments where they are interacting.

- Kirby Ferguson said: "Everything is really a remix and a better way to conceive of creative outcomes; most innovation is built on the ideas of others."

- Our perceptions of wanted and unwanted outcomes is a significant factor affecting performance. Understanding human development is a key skill; misunderstandings bring on some disastrous consequences.

Modernizing Approaches to Learning is organized into six overlapping sections:

Part One: Changes

Part Two: Counterintuitive Rethinking

Part Three: Lowering Frustration and Intimidation

Part Four: Insights

Part Five: Strategies and Studies

Part Six: Extra Credit

NOTES: Throughout the book I have left areas where you can jot down your thoughts. It's your book, go ahead and write in it!

_____

_____

_____

_____

_____

_____

_____

_____

Part One

Changes

"Any new view is first attacked as absurd! Then it is accepted to be true, but insignificant, then finally it seems to be important; so important that its adversaries will claim that they discovered it."
William James

"The goal of education is better conceived as helping students develop the tools and strategies needed to acquire the knowledge necessary to think productively. The meaning of knowledge has shifted from being able to remember and repeat information to being able to find and use information."
Nobel Lauriat Herbert Simon (1996)

History of the Learning Sciences

The Cambridge Handbook of the Learning Sciences was published in 2006, edited by Keith Sawyer.

This 600-page resource has contributions and research from sixty-two leading universities including: MIT, Harvard, Washington University, Georgia Tech, Northwestern, Michigan, Carnegie Mellon, Vanderbilt, California, Pittsburg, Drexel, Hawaii, North Texas, Stanford, Southern Illinois, Indiana, Utrecht, and several research centers including: Ontario Institute for Studies in Education, Adobe Systems for Technology in Learning and the Institute of Education, London.

In the late 1980s scientists who studied learning realized that they needed to develop new scientific approaches that would go beyond what each individual science was capable of uncovering and began to collaborate with others fields of science. *The Learning Sciences* was born in 1991, when their first international conference was held and the *Journal of Learning Sciences* was published.

The Learning Sciences are made up of cognitive science, educational psychology, computer science, anthropology, neuroscience, biology, sociology and other fields of science. *The Learning Sciences* is an interdisciplinary field that studies teaching and learning with the goal of enhancing learning environments, allowing people to learn more quickly, deeply and more efficiently.

Between 2003 and 2006 the National Science Foundation funded nearly 100 million dollars in grants to accelerate the development of *The Learning Sciences*. Today more and more individuals in and out of education realize that the research emerging from *The Learning Sciences* has great potential for improving teaching and learning.

For example: research has discovered that computers (technology) only benefit acts of learning when they take into account what is known about how we learn.

In the 19th and 20th centuries we did not know a great deal about how people actually learn. Approaches to learning were being designed on assumptions that had never been scientifically evaluated. These traditional approaches are known as "instructionism" (Paport 1993).

Beginning in the 1970s, research uncovered that most approaches to learning and teaching were deeply flawed. In the 1990s, after 20 years of research, learning scientists had reached a consensus on some basic facts about learning and teaching. This consensus was published by the United States National Research Council (see Branford, Brown, Cocking 2000).

Both factual and procedural knowledge are only useful when a person knows which situation to apply them in and how to modify them (flexible knowledge – portable skills) for each new situation beyond a learning environment. (This is an important insight!)

Students can only learn deeper conceptual understanding by <u>actively</u> participating in their own learning in ways that transform to real world skills (i.e.: self-discovery and self-evaluation).

The best way to learn is in environments that build on existing knowledge and past experiences. When approaches to learning do not engage prior knowledge, misconceptions will be engaged in real world situations. We all learn better when we are given the opportunity to reflect and express our developing insights (without criticisms).

Today there are new, more efficient ways to approach acts of learning and teaching.

<u>For Teachers</u> – Learning sciences can help enhance learning environments.

<u>For Parents</u> – Learning sciences can inform why instruction is failing and which alternatives are available from learning sciences.

<u>For Administrators</u> – Learning sciences can bring schools into the 21st century.

<u>For Policy Makers</u> – Learning sciences can help them see strengths and weaknesses in programs, teachers, and curricula.

<u>For Educational Researchers</u> – Learning sciences uncover insights that show how to participate in building meaningful learning approaches in the future.

When discussing the nature of learning, we are talking about behavior modification.

"We all want to be good accomplishers."
Dr. Joe Dispenza

If acts of learning had hearts and souls these would be located in the approaches being used to transfer information from a source to a receiver. The approach to learning is the life blood and is an emotional influence on acts of learning. How information is being shared shapes the quality of learning that is possible. I repeat, how information is being shared shapes the quality of learning that is possible.

It is this reality about learning that this book addresses by making suggestions for moving beyond many traditional views about teaching and learning. Modernized approaches to learning have a framework that puts more attention on the ***process of learning and what students do*** and less attention on what a teacher may know about the subject matter.

In her book, *Design for How People Learn*, Julie Diksen made a valuable suggestion to teachers and students; "In most learning situations it is assumed that the gap (what is missing) is information. Having information doesn't accomplish much by itself. You want students to know what to do with that information. **If the only thing a student is missing is information, then your job is actually pretty easy."**

The foundation for learning is based on a cell's ability to hold information (i.e.: make chemical notes) and put it to use in a productive manner. The cells are always exchanging information to solve problems. This process is based on the central nervous system's interactions (workable and unworkable) with the environment. Information gained in the present and information from prior experiences come together within the brain's network of cell connections to make sense and give meaning to new data.

When we get-it, learn-it, or do-it, the brain has gotten it and error adjustments for future reference. Over time the human race has survived and developed through trial and error adjustments that were often unconsciously accessed for their value.

What's New?

There is something new on the scene, neuroscience, which is accumulating knowledge about the mind-brain connection to learning at an explosive rate. **The process of sharing and finding information is being modernized!**

It comes as no surprise that human beings can experience learning, change and improve. On the other hand, insights into why meaningful learning does or does not occur can be a surprisingly counter-intuitive view into the nature of learning.

Consider the following questions about learning and add your own questions!

- How do our emotions influence learning?
- What should we know about non-conscious learning?
- How do context and environment influence learning?
- Does new information always have to make sense and have meaning before it will be encoded in long-term memory?
- Does the transfer of information consciously travel directly from a provider to a receiver of information?

- What makes the approach to learning developmentally appropriate?

This book does not directly address these questions sequentially. Any insights gained from these questions have value because their collective interconnected strength illuminates how one goes from not knowing to knowing. Approaches to learning become more brain-compatible by allowing everything that can influence learning (both consciously and non-consciously) to seamlessly support acts of learning.

For example, learning behavior is activated in accordance with an individual's emotions and their past experiences. The brain is constantly traveling through time pulling fragments of the past into the present. Without the past we would have no idea who we are. This is the difference between knowing danger and safety and the key to a human being's entire existence.

What you are reading here is not about a magic pill for learning, or as Terry Doyle, chief instructor at the faculty center for Teaching and Learning at Ferris State University put it, about "tricking students into remembering what teachers want them to remember."

The hope here is to have readers gain insights about the practice of "doing" learning, a philosophy that wants to help students develop "learning to think" and the ability to find options. Learning how something works may be more useful than knowing that it just exists. We all know that learning exists and the results can be recognized. But knowing *how* learning happens or is suppressed may be more useful than just knowing that it exists.

"There are more effective approaches to building long-term retention than simple repetition. Traditional instruction approaches focus heavily on content. Concerns about the learning experience, making it meaningful, memorable and motivational, may not even enter into the discussion. Our educational traditions aren't working well. It is time to work smarter." Milchadu Allen, Ph.D

A major aim of a modernized approach to learning is to prepare students for flexible adaptation and use of new learning in new environments – ones beyond the setting in which it was learned. The ultimate aim is to support efforts to prepare students for acquiring the tools to access information for use in a diverse set of circumstances.

Quotes from Joseph Pear's book, *The Science of Learning*

"It is important to rethink what is taught; how it is taught; and how learning is assessed."

"Our findings have a solid research base and strong implications for how we should teach."

"Learning principles are now available to guide the selection of strategies. It is a mistake to be performance-oriented rather than learning-oriented."

"With knowledge of how people learn, approaches to learning can more purposefully choose the design and structure of use to accomplish their goals."

Meaningful learning is more about removing barriers and less about getting something right.

Many centuries ago the ink dried on how the nature of learning operates, but we are still uncovering more insights into this natural process every day. One of the valuable insights is that **learn-and-develop** approaches have been found to be more useful than **teach-to-fix to get-it-right approaches**.

Learn-and-develop approaches in real world environments operate as if they were an award-winning history major, using information from past experiences and prior knowledge to support new learning.

Professor Monisha Pasupathi, author of *How We Learn*, pointed out that "misconceptions about learning are based on imperfect understanding of people as learners." Question? Do we want to have a vested interest in just providing subject content, or a vested interest in the process of learning and applying information with know-how skills?

Investing in human capital with efficient approaches to education has always been a sound choice. Let's move on under the assumption that everyone, including myself, would like to enhance his or her ability to learn. Would a fundamental rethinking about learning improve the pace of progress for students of all ages and subjects? Are there cultural misconceptions when it comes to how mankind *best* learns? Sound studies and respected research from cognitive psychology, behavioral science, educational neuroscience and other disciplines mentioned here would answer these questions with a yes!

My Journey

From time to time all professionals look back at their own career journey. As you ponder your own, I would like to share my journey with you.

I have enjoyed and feel privileged to have been teaching since the late 1960s. I have never seen myself as a perfect teacher, but have learned that human beings are competent, efficient learners. One of the ironies of doing the work of an instructor, a parent, coach, educator or employer, is that the more one learns the more one realizes how much more there is to know. I consider myself to be very fortunate; by some standards I have had success as a teacher, but any progress I may have made is founded mostly on what I have learned from others.

I had no first hand insights into what most individuals believe about learning, but after two decades of a curious voyage that included attending seminars and workshops, reading books, journals, and research papers, I now feel that what many believe about learning should be rethought. The mind-brain connection to learning is often side-stepped and studies have demonstrated the dire consequences of not using brain-compatible information delivery systems.

Over the last 20 years I have had many opportunities to gather insights from respected researchers into the brain's connection to learning. It is now my view that lessons are really not given but they are gained and acquired through personal experiences in smart, safe, playful learning environments. **It seems that the way information is presented to receivers is more than important.** ***"Life is a journey and the brain is its major mode of transportation!"***

A Change

Although I began teaching in the mid-1960s, I now see myself as more of a guide, a facilitator, a coach, or a "leanest," who is doing his best to support an individual's natural ability to learn and apply information. I no longer see myself as an evaluator of outcomes.

During the early 1980s, I had the good fortune to receive some recognition and awards for my work as a teacher. It was during these years that I began to question why some individuals who were spending time with me (a perceived expert) were not reaching what I thought was their potential and learning at an acceptable pace. What was missing from my approach to teaching?

That was the question I began to ask myself one spring morning as I waited for students to arrive. I said to myself, "You have my curiosity, now you will have my attention."

After becoming aware of what respected research from modern science was uncovering about the mind-brain connection to learning, I began to rethink the approach to teaching I had used for twenty years. I then changed from using the dead language of what I call a teacher-centered **teach-to-fix and get-it-right approach,** to using an active student-centered **learn-and-develop approach**

Why was an award-winning instructor changing his approach to teaching? Because at the time what I was sharing with students was based only on the subject content information that was available at the time. **I was teaching with just one side of the story (subject content), without an insight into the nature of *learning* that content.** Steven Pinker, then at M.I.T., Howard Gardner of Harvard, and many other leading educators would have said of my work at that time – "Teacher yes, educator no!" I, and others, have found that just giving individuals information is unsatisfying, when compared to helping students learn how to learn.

> "That teaching strategies (a.k.a approaches to learning) overcome all other factors by significant margins, is the most stunning finding to come out of education research in the past decade."

Readers should know when I was first exposed to studies about the nature of learning; my own biased thinking caused me to doubt and question. These new to me views about teaching and learning were non-traditional and foreign to how I was currently approaching teaching. These insights that were new to me were making me question the value of some long held cultural assumptions that were influencing teaching, but were not taking into consideration the nature of learning – A LARGE OVERSIGHT. This change in my approach to instruction was not the only observation noted. It was also noted that the students who were spending time in this modernized learning environment were now learning faster and retaining information and skills longer.

In the past, the main focus of my approach to teaching was to become subject content rich. So, from the mid-1960s through the 1980s, I constantly tried to gather all the subject content information I could from books, workshops, seminars, journals and observing other teachers, all as part of my efforts to grow as an instructor. I later became aware that a very important, perhaps the most important, component, was missing from my approach to teaching – insights into the mind-brain connection to learning. "The real educator, in fact, lets nothing else be learned but learning."[7]

After I gained the insight that the culture of trying to teach is different from the culture of helping someone to learn, I realized that I had several misconceptions about the process of learning that needed to be rethought. *I would become determined to start researching the nature of learning and this would captivate my professional development.*

This was the start of my journey to modernize the structure and substance of the approach to teaching that I had been using since 1966. I realized that I didn't need to know more subject content, but I clearly needed to know more about the mind-brain connection to *learning* that content if I was going to grow as a teacher. I feel fortunate to have been made aware that I needed to know more about the nature of learning.

At times it has felt like a lonely journey and a good way to slow down my career. As I was moving off the topic of just teaching subject content and what other teachers were doing, into researching the brain's connection to learning, I was told there was little interest in the research I was doing – which is no longer the case in the 21st century.

Today, almost every university in the world is doing research about the brain's connection to learning. Educators are taking courses on this topic; books, articles and papers are being published on a constant basis filled with insights about the nature of learning that were not available in the past.

As Eric Jensen suggested, learning should be approached "with the brain in mind." In the past you could say I had a lesson plan for the content I was teaching, but my plan for helping students learn that content efficiently needed to be rethought and modernized.

---

[7] Martin Heidegger quote

Warning: Some long held beliefs about learning have the support of good politics which new insights and new research can be missing. Unfortunately good politics, existing culture, or personal bias can keep what has been used in the past alive. Putting politics aside, it is time to exchange 20th century teaching for 21st century learning.

When seen through the eyes of the mind-brain connection to learning, I was unknowingly making some poor decisions during the first twenty years I was teaching. My approach was not keeping up with current research into the nature of learning.

According to research, the culture and customs of some current approaches to learning should be rethought. *How information is delivered matters.* There are always environmental influences on learning. Information delivery systems are important environmental components of the learning process. With a brain-compatible approach to learning, something different becomes something more valuable.

Recently some who are researching the mind-brain connection to learning have referred to many traditional (but out of date) approaches to learning as crude. This is especially true when new research from science about learning is not taken into consideration by teachers and students. By today's standards during the 19th and 20th centuries we did not know a great deal about the nature of learning. Fortunately this has been changing in the 21st century.

Many organizations and university research centers have revealed that there are some common assumptions about learning that are incorrect. These organizations include:

- The Office of Education Research and Improvement of the US Department of Education
- Harvard University Graduate School of Educations Connecting the Mind-Brain and Education Institute which

recently committed to helping improve the learning experiences for everyone through research into the brain's connection to learning

- Vanderbilt University Peabody College of Education National Center on Quality Teaching and Learning is building new pathways for innovation, research and reform in education
- University of Washington's Institute for Learning and Brain Sciences is currently researching the brain mechanisms that underline the windows of opportunity for learning
- Columbia University Teacher's College has a vision to Have educational opportunities unlocking the wonders of human potential

A Letter

After he learned that I was compiling research about the brain's connection to learning, renowned brain scientist Professor Stephen Yazulla sent me a letter with some suggestions and insights on this topic. To have him take an interest in supporting my effort to learn more about the nature of learning was more than fortunate.

We had several discussions about enhancing learning environments by applying research from several fields of science. Then, one day, he said he would put some thoughts on paper and send them to me.

He opened his letter with, "I agree with you wholeheartedly about having to change the culture of traditional approaches to learning. I have taken as a starting point your statement that, 'brain-compatible approaches' to learning lead to positive emotional responses during learning." He went on, "what I have done is list areas that have scientific bases that support the above statement."

His letter listed several elements that were supported by research for achieving brain-compatible approaches to learning as those that:

- Involve multiple sensory and motor systems in learning a task. Writing down notes by hand – and verbally stating them is more effective for learning than simply thinking about them. (A seamless combination of vision, sound, feel, and thoughts supports learning.)
- Take breaks between sessions; do not cram; particularly if shifting topics. (I have seen research that suggests changing the context every 15 minutes will enhance learning.)
- Mild stress prior to an event inspires learning. (Excited to take part.)
- Minimize distractions any competing sensory inputs will interfere with learning; in particular sounds. (Should golfers have headsets on when training? Research says no!)
- Allow choices and decisions by students and their consequences, support learning. (Self-regulation and self-discovery enhance learning.)

Professor Yazulla then suggested learning more about several components of learning: novel or new situations; context; acts of predicting; and how they influence learning outcomes. He then said that in reality every situation we encounter is always changing or is novel. He pointed out that it is non-conscious predictions that play out in scenarios for: costs and gains; present and future; success and failure, all of which eventually lead to our choices and decisions. The brain operates through and by predictions; "if this, then that." The brain is always associating new information with prior experiences.

He went on to say that in each act of planning, or revision, there is a learning process. It is interesting that both elation and disappointment are associated with emotional and physiological responses that are similar. For example; for both there is an increased heart rate, flushing of skin, fist pumping or fist punching.

Professor Yazulla pointed out that if we want to experience brain-compatible learning the culture that is embedded with the notion that "winning isn't everything; it is the only thing" has to be rethought. He pointed out this view places enormous value on winning and contempt for losing and unwanted outcomes.

"The goal therefore (to experience brain-compatible learning) seems to be to change the attitude toward mistakes or unwanted outcomes. Here is where seeing the error as opportunity comes in. Rather than being berated for a failure, one should be encouraged to do it again, while learning from past experiences."
David Brooks

The parents of brain-compatible learning are unwanted outcomes, or inconsistencies because they birth learning.

"What I have learned is teachers can make learning interesting, fun, exciting, challenging or they can make it boring, defeating, painful, and useless. My best teachers were not only encouraging and supportive; they also taught me how to learn."
Professor Terry Doyle

The neurological changes in the brain's wiring from unwanted outcomes (inconsistencies), likely have some adaptive advantage for survival. The goal then is to mute the negative response to failure by redefining unwanted outcomes as an opportunity to learn.

Moving beyond the thoughts that Professor Yazulla's shared with me, my insight is to see unwanted outcomes as natural inconsistencies in performances. These unwanted outcomes do not need fixing; they are just a natural component of performing in any walk of life. The aim is to become functional, without being misled by the idea of perfection. (See Inconsistency is Valuable and Failure vs. Feedback sections.)

Experimental education environments engage the whole human being as physical, social, cognitive, emotional and educational needs are being nurtured with a constructively positive approach.

Over time the brain has wired itself for success, not failure. We are not wired, predisposed, or biologically primed to fail tests, have accidents, or make poor decisions. Our ability to thrive and survive is what our ancestors passed on from the first moment that living organisms came into being.

There has always been an ongoing effort to improve learning and the results this process was producing. New suggestions, new methods and new theories for approaches to learning have come and gone over time. It is fair to say that there was some good to be found in most of them.

It is also fair to say that, at their foundation, these past theories and methods did not have the advantage of the new insights from research about how the brain learns. In the past, when ideas about learning were developed, research from modern neuroscience about the nature of learning was not readily available.

The view here is that approaches to learning should seek to develop individuals who become confident, eager, self-motivated learners; individuals who are independent thinkers, curious, and self-reliant; learners who gain self-knowledge, while fulfilling their potential with open minds. It appears that meaningful learning comes from the best ingredients on earth; curiosity, imagination and improvisational skills and *not* from criticisms or corrections.

The reality is that the term "lesson" reveals no more about the quality of learning taking place than the word "restaurant" reveals about the quality of food. When progress is slow, keep the following insight in mind, *"We begin to express fulfillment as soon as we choose to create environments promoting us to do so."* Bob Staples

What if there were information delivery systems and strategies that educators, sports coaches, parents, and employers could use that were significantly more efficient for helping individuals learn faster and retain information longer than the approaches they were currently using?

What if there was a way for learning to occur more quickly, to be retained longer, and to be more intuitively relevant?

What if there was a way to avoid individuals being emotionally consumed with getting something right or wrong when they were learning?

What if there was a way for learning environments to lower the kind of stress that fragments progress?

What if there was a way for a learning environment to be fail free?

Modernizing Approaches to Learning was compiled to offer insights from neuroscience about updated approaches to learning, but with an old world view. Again, keep an open mind as some of these new insights are counterintuitive and non-traditional approaches suggesting a minimalist approach to a full education. By the way, minds are like parachutes, they both work best when open!

David Perkins, Harvard Graduate School of Education states, "There is new emerging framework that is bringing to Harvard a lot of surprises and eye opening insights about the brain's connection to learning and it appears that this is the way we should think about learning. The evidence no longer supports many long held traditional approaches to learning."

The *culture* of the approach that is being used to transfer information from educator to student, parent to child, sports coach/instructor to player, employer to employee will determine if meaningful learning is even possible.

In *The Seven Sins of Memory,* by Daniel Schacter, it is noted that there is nothing more expensive than a closed mind, with a "personal bias" being listed as one of the main reasons for not remembering.

Unfortunately, one of our most important gifts from nature, the ability to learn, can be fragmented. Hopefully, what is being put forward here will help readers protect and enhance this natural potential for learning. Today, questions about the design and value of some approaches to learning are being raised by respected cognitive scientists.

Suggestion!
Don't change your vision; change your way of getting there.

When the term "approach to learning," is referred to as brain-compatible, some of the qualities include:

- Emotionally supportive (most are not)
- Physically safe (some are not)
- Developmentally appropriate (many are not)
- Give students choices (few do)
- Avoid judgments (most do not)
- Free of negative criticism (few are)
- Find unwanted outcomes useful for improving (most do not)
- Change poor insights (few do)

A short story about learning based on book titles!

A Journey to Wisdom and *Peak Learning* with *The Power of Play* finds *The Everyday Genius* in all of us. *The Talent Code* found in *The Naked Brain* uses *The Art of Awareness to Know What We Know*. These *Creative Powers* avoid the *Seven Senses of Memory* with *A Mind of its Own* using the *Emotional Brain*.

The Bright Air and *Brilliant Fire* in *The Origins of Intelligence* uncovered by *The Science Behind What Makes Us Unique*, shows

What it Means to be Well Educated. Science, the Brain and Our Future will *Spark The Power of Ideas* and *The Engine of Reason from Neurons to Neighborhoods. A Mind Wide Open* guides *The Playful Brain.*

Between Parent and Child, Teacher and Child, Learning Together with Brain Friendly Strategies is Activating the Desire to Learn with Habits of the Mind that say *I Want to Learn, Please Stop Teaching Me* while *Exchanging 20th Century Teaching for 21st Century Learning.*

Places for Learning, Places for Joy all move in the direction of a *Theory of Instruction* filled with *Fantasy and Feeling in Education* that uncovers *The Power of Ideas. The Smart Swarm of Peak Learning* and *The Edge of Possibility* are the *Anatomy of the Miracle* found in the *Situation and the Person.*

Emotional Intelligence is the *Heart of the Mind, Reframing a Spark* that reveals *Working knowledge* and *The Art of Being* while using *A Brain for All Seasons. The Celebration of Neurons* opens *The Tree of Knowledge* with *Multiple Intelligence* leading to *The Every Day Genius* and *Peak Learning.*

The Power of Now creates *Mindstorms* that help *How People Learn* while *Making Good Brains Better* as *The Art of Learning* develops *A Well Educated Mind* as *The Playful Brain is* uncovering *Cooperative Learning* with *A Mind Wide Open* for *Thinking Creatively.*

Bibliography for these titles located on page 230

A Reverse Paradigm Shift

A paradigm shift is most often described as an idea that *thinks out of the box* and goes forward beyond what is accepted as the norm, questioning the value of traditional ideas. The ideas and suggestions posed in this book question some long held beliefs about learning, but not by going forward outside the box. Perhaps what has been compiled here could be seen as a *reverse* **paradigm shift,** one that is offering information by going back to what has always been nature's plan for efficient learning. By revisiting what has always been available to us, we can move forward and experience the joy of meaningful learning.

Insights Into the Brain's Learning System

It is said that one of the most valuable achievements of modern science is uncovering new insights into the nature of learning and the mind-brain connection to this process. This connection is referred to as "our brain learning system," by Todd Maddox, University of Texas, Austin. One of the many books now available about the brain's connection to learning is *Understanding the Brain: The Birth of a Learning Science*, published by The Center for Education Research and Innovation. Insights into how the brain decodes, encodes and recalls information are among the most meaningful discoveries made in science.

When meaningful learning is not being encoded perhaps some evolutionary principles from the nature of learning are being side-stepped and not put to use in favor of some popular customs and cultural views. Unfortunately this is happening in the 21st century even though data from modern science has shown that acts of learning can be enhanced by using insights about the mind-brain connection to the nature of learning. **Learning is a thought exercise and not a memory task.**

"The power of thought is the magic of the mind."
Lord Byron

Customs and Culture

Culture is part of the environment in which learning takes place.

Customs and cultural views can change quickly, especially when it comes to ideas about education and learning. Over time views about education have changed many times, often in the span several years.

On the other hand, it's taken millions of years to accomplish evolutionary changes to the human race. For example, the nature of learning and our ability to adapt to ever changing real world environments are natural skills that have always existed. It is fair to say that the human brain that discovered the use of fire, the wheel, language and other tools of survival is essentially the same brain found in human beings today.

Unfortunately, there are some long held customs and cultural views that are negatively influencing natural acts of learning when the principles of learning, passed on by evolution, are being side-stepped. **At first, information may appear complex, but learning it does not have to be.**

Gaining insights into the natural nature of learning and the mind-brain connection to this process is a journey in two directions at the same time. One direction is moving away from damaging approaches to learning and the other is moving in the direction of experiencing long-term learning. Meaningful learning is supported by moving toward self-discovery and self-reliance skills and away from customs that foster poor self-image and lack of self-confidence.

There will be an immediate enhancement of approaches to learning – a topic that has pedigree as old as time – when insights from modern science are taken into consideration.

The gateway to learning is our brain and any information delivery system is enhanced when it is compatible with the brain's connection to that process of learning. Some of what follows is repetitive, but learning is supported by repercussions and my aim is to help readers learn what they may not know about how learning works.

The 1990s has been referred to as the "Decade of the Brain." It was during these years that scientists and educators learned more about the brain's connection to learning than at any other time in the history of research. We now know there are some keys to learning and teaching that were not recognized in the past and they will be discussed here. The unintentional consequences of overlooking them will also be addressed. Staying on a positive path to progress requires more than accurate information (which is just one side of the story). Insights into the steps and stages of effective learning are also useful.

It has been pointed out that we do not need data-driven instruction. What is needed is *knowledge-driven learning* in the direction of know-how skills. Data is a way of expressing information such as numbers, charts, and statistics that have little value in and of themselves. On the other hand, knowledge is applying information appropriately to a contextual situation.

Ideas

Ideas are invisible and weightless, with no external physical substance, but they have the power to make changes, improvements and enhance what exists. Ideas also have the ability to prevent changes and improvements.

Many of the ideas from science in this book have started to change how learning is being viewed in the 21st century. These ideas about the brain's connection to learning are the very substance of modernized approaches to learning that support learning faster and retaining information and skills longer.

"Students are only learning-disabled in some learning environments"
David Rose, Harvard Graduate School of Education

The Brain, A Learner
A Mind-On, Hands-On System

"Our brain contains a mental toolbox developed over millions of years of evolution to help our ancestors survive and reproduce in challenging environments."[8] The brain is a problem solving, self-learning organ.

At some point everyone has been a teacher and a student. That said, any parent, employer, coach, student or educator would enhance how they transfer information to others by answering these two questions: What should teachers and students know about the nature of learning? How does one go from not knowing to knowing?

"Man can learn nothing without going from the known to the unknown."
Claude Bermard

There is a difference in learning information that supports the skills of creating and inventing and learning just for the sake of knowing that information. Brain-compatible approaches to learning develop know-how skills for use in ever changing real world environments.

The value of discussing the brain connection to learning needs no defense. Without our internal mind-brain activity what could the human race have accomplished, including meaningful learning, the ultimate survival skill? "Learning to learn is the most

---

[8] *Mind Wide Open*, by Steven Johnson, p.9

important skill of our times."[9] What can be done before, during and after acts of learning to enhance the enjoyment of the learning process? We now know there are many strategies we can use to enhance learning.

There are no poor learners, only poorly designed approaches to learning that can share confusing messages.

Perhaps there should be a term for things that are so much a part of our lives that we never think about them. When was the last time you thought about the brain and how it influences our daily lives and our ability to learn? Honest answer. I know I was unaware of the brain's connection to learning for the first twenty years I was teaching.

Some approaches to learning are at war with the obvious. Often there is a gap between what providers of information know and their ability to support an approach for learning that information. **How information is being shared with receivers often causes gaps in learning.**

A car mechanic's job is to repair cars. A lawyer's job is to provide legal help. A doctor's job is to restore health and an educator's job is to help individuals learn.

Mechanics, attorneys and doctors, normally know both sides of the story. They not only know subject content information, they also have the know-how skills to use that content to accomplish their job in ever changing environments.

On the other hand some teachers and other providers of information can be aware of accurate information but they often do not know enough about the brain's connection to the natural nature of learning to help an individual experience meaningful learning.

---

[9] Ronald Gross of Columbia University at the "Summit for Life Long Learning."

Thus they have tools for only one side of their job; providing information without insights for learning that information.

The hope here is to create an epidemic of meaningful learning by understanding that when we approach learning smarter, we help others and ourselves learn faster and retain information and skills longer.

I have written other books and ended my last book with the statement "To Be Continued..." This book also ends with "To Be Continued..." For we never know what the future may hold. Most of what is being put forward here about approaches to learning was not available before the late 1980s. Research has made some illuminating suggestions for using a proactive positive approach for enhancing learning potential that starts by avoiding negative judgments and criticisms.

Some of the topics discussed here include: mind-brain, acts of learning, learning environments, memory, emotions, context, self-discovering and self-evaluation.

On September 28, 1919, Albert Einstein at the request of the *London Times* wrote an article about his "Theory of Relativity." He started the article by writing, "in order to grasp the nature of this theory, one needs first of all to become acquainted with some of the principles on which it is based."

I am following Einstein's lead. This book was written to help individuals who have an interest in the topic of learning become more acquainted with some of the basic principles behind brain-compatible information delivery systems. While learning can have the element of wonderment, it is a wide range of actual cell connections in our nervous system that supports meaningful learning.

Brain-compatible approaches to learning are not a fad or just another educational experiment. They represent meaningful changes from traditional approaches to learning based on the brain's connection to learning. "Though we often say that we learn in school, learning actually takes place in the brain," said

Kenneth Wesson whose work in education, learning and teaching spans four decades.

A century and a half ago (1879), Brooks Adams, a member of the Boston school board wrote, "Knowing a child cannot be taught everything, it is best to teach them how to learn." He then noted that most schools had no connection to such an approach. That is a statement that often rings true today.

In the book *Bright Air, Brilliant Fire*, author Nobel Laureate Gerald M. Edelman spoke about some very exciting news, "we are at the beginning of a neuro-scientific revolution and on the threshold of knowing how we know." Edelman went on, "I think this subject is the most important one imaginable." Who could disagree with him? Human development and meaningful approaches to learning are one in the same.

As Kurt W. Fischer (Harvard University) and Mary Helen Immordino-Yong (University of South California) pointed out in their paper *The Fundamental Importance of the Brain and Learning for Education,* "People learn. Learning is fundamental to us human beings. It is the specialization that we use to become fully human."

I found the following quotes in the book *The Brain, a guide for educators, parents and teachers* (edited by Sheryl Feinstein).

- "It is irresponsible to ignore what is being learned about the brain; it helps us make better decisions in offering a quality education experience."
- "Universities across the country are endorsing this area of study. Their programs now include a combination of both the content areas of learning (subjects) and the cognitive neuroscience of learning and their objectives."

It is very important that approaches to learning move the

perception of unwanted outcomes beyond seeing them as something shameful in need of fixing, and have them recognized as valuable feedback for future reference. Without unworkable outcomes and misperceptions, there would be little or no meaningful learning. Brain-compatible approaches to learning recognize that the past experiences of unworkable outcomes are more valuable for new learning than workable outcomes, sometimes by as much as a 5 to 1 ratio.

Approaches to learning send emotional, chemical signals to students and some signals make learning possible and unfortunately there are signals that can make learning more difficult than nature intended it to be. Learning is an emotional, chemical process based mostly on prior knowledge.

Studies show, there are often gaps between students and approaches to learning that can be reduced by rethinking some long held cultural influences. In the late 1980s I started to realize that I had to re-educate myself about the nature of learning, which has been my journey for over two decades.

One of the most recent opportunities to re-educate myself about learning was attending classes at Harvard University's Graduate School of Education. The classes were held in Harvard's Connecting Mind-Brain to Education Institute, directed by Kurt Fischer and some of the reasons for not learning were discussed, including these obstacles:

- Students were judged
- No opportunity for students to self-discover or self-evaluate
- Students were not given choices
- The way information is presented to students
- Information was not important to students
- How questions are asked of students
- Information given to students was not based on a concept

- Misconceptions in students' minds
- Information was counter intuitive to students
- Information was given to students without metaphors
- Students were given more details than needed

What we have learned from many foresighted scientists and educators has led us to a more complete picture of the nature of learning. It is a model that does not require all of the mysteries of the brain be known before it is useful for developing insights which can enhance approaches to learning.

By recognizing that the brain has a connection to learning, the unacceptable results of not keeping the brain in mind can be filtered out of any learning environment. Simply put, we learn according to how the brain wired itself for learning. The original construction evolved over time into today's brain as more connections in brain wiring were created during every new generation.

Knowing what something is *not* may often be more useful than knowing what it *is*. When it comes to the brain's information processing skills, to know that something *is not* is important and we have modern science to thank for these insights.

The theory of learning that is being discussed here is grounded in brain-compatible information delivery systems. Research evaluates the value of any theory by asking questions including:

- Does the theory reflect the real world of human beings?
- Is the theory supported by convincing evidence?
- Does the theory explain past, present, and future outcomes?
- Is the theory open to new research?
- Is the theory understandable?
- Is the theory emotionally self-satisfying?

The theory of learning that is discussed here meets all of these questions with a positive response.

If meaningful learning is to be experienced, just sharing accurate subject content will be much too limiting. A topic must be moved in and out of a variety of different contexts in a way that it will connect with prior knowledge. This approach is taking the brain's connection to learning into consideration; just sharing subject content does not.

Navigating barriers and resistance to accepting the value of what modern science is uncovering about the brain's connection to learning leads to a thrilling metamorphosis of a culture found in traditional but out of date views of a learning process. This may seem like finding something new, but the nature of learning is filled with elements that might not always be appreciated although they are as old as the life of the first living organisms.

Moving away from confrontational approaches in the direction of cooperative approaches will illuminate, not eliminate, that value of democratic approaches to learning that avoid a form of dictatorship found in some approaches to learning.

Within our predisposed abilities is the natural ability to experience meaningful learning without *trying* to learn. When this reality is recognized the opportunity to reach one's potential as a teacher or student is being supported.

Topic Learning

There have been decades of research vested in the question of how learning **best** happens. There have also been millions of words written and spoken about this topic. But there is a very short answer to the question of how do human beings learn: **we start the learning process by taking in information from our senses.**

Perhaps we can say that in any learning environment (schools, sports instruction, homes, business seminars, etc.), the responsibility of providers of information is to support the most efficient way of acquiring, remembering and using new information.

Now that we have an answer, (we start learning by taking in information), we could say that is the end of the story. But let's keep going and ask some questions about taking in information:

- How and where was the new information provided?
- In what context was the information provided?
- Did the information come in the form of a criticism, judgment, or correction?
- Did the information come from focusing on a result or becoming more aware of the process of learning?
- Was the information provided by a perceived expert or gained through self-discovery?
- Was the information introduced through a metaphor?
- Was the information connected to the receiver's past experiences?
- Was the information uncovered when the approach to learning was helping individuals invent outcomes, or when the approach was providing answers?
- Was the information given in a physically and emotionally SAFE environment?
- Was the approach to learning information using a SMART approach?
- Was the information given in a PLAYFUL environment?
- Did the information come in the form of how-to directions or from what-to-do information?
- Did the information come from changing insights or from trying to change an unwanted outcome?
- Was the information just beyond the current information base and skill level of the receiver of information?

- Did the information arrive during a random, ever-changing approach to learning or in a structured, detailed approach?
- Did information come from giving individuals choices or from giving answers or directions?

Yes, we learn by taking in information, but how, where, and when was the new information made available to the student? What stimulates or suppresses the behavioral mechanisms of experiencing meaningful learning?

What has been written here fully recognizes that science is only a tool that can uncover insights that support meaningful learning, but science is not the creator of learning. It is individuals; in their own unique ways, that create acts of meaningful learning.

Before reading on let's provide an interactive opportunity. Please evaluate the following statements about learning as true or false based on your current views.

1   Meaningful learning environments are also social environments. T. F.
2   Learning facts can be less useful than developing skills. T. F.
3   You should try to fix unwanted outcomes when learning. T. F.
4   You should try to get something right when learning. T. F.
5   The conscious mind is more valuable than the non-conscious mind when learning. T. F.
6   Focusing on how-to directions from a perceived expert is more useful when learning than becoming aware of what-to-do. T. F.
7   Focusing on how to move one's body is more useful than learning what the current environment requires us to do with an object. T. F.

8 Approaching learning with general, just in-the-ball-park concepts are not as useful as an approach that uses specific details. T. F.

9 Long-term learning is encoded after a lesson and often during sleep. T. F.

10 Expert models are best used as models to copy. T. F.

11 Praise can be punishment. T. F.

12 A master of anything was first a master of learning. T. F.

13 Actions of parents, employers, coaches, educators should make individuals feel smart. T. F.

14 Being taught that what a perceived expert believes is the "right way" is less useful than learning to develop your own approach. T. F.

15 A conformity approach to progress is more useful than a random approach. T. F.

16 Often learning is making an unconscious shift from a belief to a fact. T. F.

17 When learning anything, both workable and unworkable outcomes have value – with unworkable outcomes more useful. T. F.

18 New learning is encoded as the safety of the environment and the emotional state of the students are simultaneously evaluated by the brain's past experiences. T. F.

(Answers: 1T. 2T.3 F. 4F. 5F. 6F. 7F. 8F. 9T. 10F. 11T. 12T. 13T. 14T. 15F. 16 T. 17T. 18T.)

"Techniques used in teaching, more important than who Teacher is."

That was the headline of an <u>Associated Press</u> story in May of 2011. The article pointed out that a study by a Nobel Prize winning physicist suggests that how you teach is more important than who does the teaching. Respected research found that interactive approaches to learning were better than a traditional lecture approach.

Approaches to learning could be described as a source and a receiver of information actively interacting. The question being discussed here is: what makes the interactions between a source and a receiver of information mind-brain-compatible for encoding meaningful learning?

Approaches to learning should help people gain an advantage they did not have. Gaining a good education can be more about acquiring insights that can enhance one's ability to construct and expand our personal know-how knowledge than about memorizing information or following how-to directions from perceived experts to fix unwanted outcomes.

Human beings are born as champion estimators. We all have a very efficient approximation system (a survival skill) that following how-to direction can suppress. Unfortunately, most individuals have been ingrained with the Puritan work ethic, "If you don't try hard, you will not succeed." Hopefully, you will come to understand that the very act of trying

> **T R Y**
>
> **T**alking and
>
> **R**idiculing
>
> **Y**ourself
>
> when learning.

brings tension and rigidity. When we obtain insights into the nature of learning, we have the freedom to learn without trying.

I now realize that trying to teach someone is different than helping individuals to learn. Modernized approaches to learning are a journey filled with self-confidence that develops into self-reliance skills. Teach-to-fix (get-it-right) approaches to learning are not only different from learn-and-develop approaches; they have been shown to be less for learning.

When it comes to learning, the main challenge is not unwanted outcomes; it is more about finding an efficient approach (bridge) for enhancing the ability to learn. A dictated curriculum put forward by a perceived expert rarely improves the ability to personally reason toward workable outcomes in real world environments. **Understanding how one goes from not knowing to knowing and putting to use new learning in ever-**

changing environments is just as important as the subject matter that individuals are learning.

It is surprising what can be overlooked about our natural ability to learn when teachers, coaches, parents, or business training programs are seen as the main source of answers for the problem to be solved (seeing options). The Committee on Learning Research and Educational Practices in America stated, "teacher-assistedenvironments that guide, motivate and support self-discovery learning are more effective than teacher-centered environments. Learning skills and education do not come from teachers."

Research about learning falls into two categories: the research and the application of those studies. Here, I have tried to join these two categories. Learning what science has uncovered about how our brain best learns, and why these findings should be taken into consideration, improves approaches to help individuals make progress.

"Many people who had difficulty learning in the past might have prospered if the new ideas about efficient instruction practices had been available."[10]

The following insights about learning have influenced what is discussed throughout this book.

1. <u>A master of anything was first a master of learning.</u> Harvard's Lawrence Hooper states, "The ultimate source of exceptional performance is exceptional learning. Therefore the question is how can we best produce exceptional learning?"
One answer: There is a smaller return on the investment of time and resources by trying to change unwanted outcomes (i.e. poor habits, poor grades), than when we enhance an individual's learning potential first, which then improves their performance potential.

---

[10] *How People Learn*, by Branford, Brown, Cocking, 2000

2. The brain is the gateway to learning. "What has been uncovered about the brain requires a fundamental change in education," says Professor Harry Chugani. "It is what somebody does in their brain and nervous system that produces a result." Tan James M.S., Ph.D

The Institute of Learning and Brain Science, University of Washington – *"We believe that the scientific study of the development of the mind-brain is the next great frontier. Discoveries about the brain's connection to learning in the next decade will be comparable to those in genetics and biotechnology." "Learning and developing happen within the web of connections in the brain."* Jean Paget, Vygotsky

3. Research has shown that learning is mostly a non-conscious process. We do not have to try to learn; we just can and do in brain-compatible learning environments. The ability to learn is a predisposed natural survival skill, passed on by evolution

Dr. Elmire Donchin, "most of our learning doesn't even require that we pay conscious attention; 99% of all learning is a non-conscious process."[11]

"People need to stop believing that they have conscious control of their actions."
David Brooks

4. Meaningful learning is based on our prior knowledge base (on old learning) and present perceptions. When new information does not connect in some way to what an individual already knows or has experienced, it is less likely to be learned. Stories and metaphors are powerful learning tools. An efficient conscious and non-conscious transfer of information connects first to our memory. Information must make sense and have meaning to the

---

[11] *Brain Facts*, p.19

receiver of information (based on our past experiences), for it to be encoded as long-term learning.

Growth and reorganization should not be seen as synonymous. Growth could be seen as gaining more information. On the other hand, reorganization could be seen as gaining new insights and points of view that differ from existing information.

The value of a piece of information is based on how one associates it.

Our ability to connect and see patterns in ideas is important to the quality of learning that we experience. Lots of links to a diversified network of past experiences can be incorporated into workable outcomes in the now, (or present). Chunks or bundles or information that may seem to bear little resemblance to the task at hand become the tools of choice for long-term learning.

5. Meaningful learning is both a chemical and emotional process. Some approaches to learning cause the release of chemicals within the brain and body that support learning. Other approaches cause the release of chemicals that can suppress meaningful learning. Learning environments should be emotionally and physically safe, smart, and playful.

The emotional state of individuals and the emotional climate and culture of the learning environment directly influence acts of learning.

Dr. John Medina, "learning is deeply affected by the emotional environment in which learning takes place."[12] "It has become evident that any portrait of human nature that ignores motivation and emotion proves to be of limited use in facilitating human learning."[13]

Emotions organize brain wiring; what seems good or bad, wanted or avoided, is created by the concepts and feelings generated by emotions. Mary Helen Immordino Yang's – University of

[12] *The Brain,* by Alexander Blade, p. 96
[13] *The Disciplined Mind,* by Howard Gardiner, p. 77

Southern California – research into emotions and learning has been ground breaking.

6. It has been shown that acts of "fixing" do not support long-term learning. Some believe because learning is about change, learning must be about fixing. Harvard's David Perkins calls unwanted outcomes, "desirable, developmental difficulties." Unwanted outcomes are a biological necessity of meaningful learning.

Focusing on what to do supports learning more efficiently than focusing on fixing unwanted outcomes. In a brain-compatible learning environment students are not seen as broken and in need of fixing. They are on a journey of development.

7. In brain-compatible learning environments there is no failure. Unworkable outcomes should be seen and used as valuable feedback for future reference. Bjork – "People learn by making and changing poor outcomes. Introducing mistakes during training is important."

8. Brain-compatible learning is not a step by step linear process. "Meaningful learning is a simultaneous activity of development, with no single component of change developing by itself. Learning is something that is happening in many different ways." Kurt Fischer, Harvard's Connecting Mind-Brain to Education Institute

9. Frequently changing the context in which learning takes place enhances learning potential.
The University of California San Diego (2000) found that re-exposing ourselves to information repeatedly for short periods of time strengthens learning. Encountering the same material in brief sessions that are spread out over time has more than doubled retention rate.

Changing the context in which information is being used often strengthens learning.

10. Approaches to learning should be developmentally appropriate, happen in context, be free of negative judgments and

use metaphors. Introduce information or skills that are just beyond current capacity.

NOTES:

_____

_____

_____

_____

_____

_____

_____

_____

_____

_____

_____

_____

_____

_____

_____

_____

_____

_____

_____

_____

_____

_____

_____

_____

_____

_____

_____

_____

Approaches to Learning and Re-Education

Chart credit *Play Golf to Learn Golf*, **by Michael Hebron**

20th Century Teach-to-fix	21st Century Learn-and-develop
Teach	**Educate**
Critical observations and judgments of outcomes	Provide positive feedback
Focus on a specified result as a goal	Focus on the learning process as the goal
Follow directions	Allow students to learn through their own experiences
Teacher has the answer	Individuals construct their own knowledge base
Students attempting to get-it-right	Students encouraged to experiment
Students show concern before they act	Students evaluate after they act
Suggest using drills to learn	Utilizes random experimentation to learn
Uses expert models	Uses learning models
Uses out of context teaching aids	Use in context environments
Uses detailed, specific information	Use just in-the-ball-park, non-specific concepts
Uses *how-to* directions	Promotes imagination, self-discovery, what-if thinking

20th Century Teach-to-fix	21st Century Learn-and-develop
Teachers are evaluators	Students self-evaluate
Uses memorization	Uses indirect preparation
Values current information	Values past experiences
Values following directions	Offers choices
Result orientated, a get-it-right environment	An investment in a students' learning potential
Focus on providing details	Uses general concepts
Try to *fix* personal habits by focusing on dogma	Focus on the design and structure of the approach to learning
Focus on subject matter	Focus on non-academic skills that support learning potential
Provide answers	Help students create useful questions
Biased	Open minded
Passive learning	Active learning
Uses details from perceived experts	Uses interactions by students
Focused on poor outcomes	Discovers poor insights
Attempt to conquer	Use cooperation
Points out failure	All outcomes are valuable feedback for future reference
Class sessions have a beginning and a finish	Learning environments are never ending

20th Century Teach-to-fix	21st Century Learn-and-develop
Are geared for providing information	Develop the capacity for finding and inventing knowledge that's personal in nature
Are judgmental	Provide acceptance
Geared for treatment	Geared for prevention
Try to teach	Coach – guide – support self-discovery
Promotes fixing	Develops enlightenment from unwanted outcomes

Approaches to learning can produce various results. The approach can either: provide the answer; provide the tools to help students find their own answer; or trigger core emotions that suppress meaningful learning.

Learn-and-develop approaches to learning use a different language than a teach-to-fix approach or a get-it-right approach. Learn-and-develop approaches uses words that are emotionally compatible with the nature of learning. The choice of words used to deliver a thought can either stimulate learning or suppress it; the latter is sometimes misinterpreted as a student's lack of skill or interest.

Words are powerful so choose them carefully!
Powerful performance enhancers
Or
Powerful curiosity and learning suppressors

Types of Pals
(Educator, Parent, Employer, Instructor, Coach)

Tom Rath, author of *Vital Friends: The People You Can't Afford to Live Without*, says friends can fall into the several categories. He points out that undoubtedly; there is a fair degree of overlap. He suggests that the following are the kinds of pals that share information in a brain-compatible positive manner.

- **Builder**: Pumps you up, motivates you, helps you see your strengths, cheers you on.
- **Champion**: Stands up for you, praises you, advocates for you when you're not around.
- **Collaborator**: Shares your interests and passions.
- **Companion**: Is always there no matter what; the person you call first when something good or bad happens.
- **Connector**: Links you up with others who share your interests or goals; extends your network.
- **Energizer**: Boosts your spirits, creates positive feelings; the person you call when you need a laugh.
- **Mind-opener**: Expands your vision, introduces you to new ideas, and challenges conventional thinking.
- **Navigator**: Shares advice and direction; helps you talk through options to find your path.

I repeat! This book is about leveraging the mind-brain connection to learning. When the goal is meaningful learning, we all need more than hope. A mind-brain-compatible approach to learning is needed. Brain-compatible also means the approach to learning is emotionally compatible for learning; emotions have the power to support or hinder learning.

The Romance Stage of Learning and Developing

This may be the most important topic in this book!

- Why do human beings want to take part in some activities and not others?
- Why do we want to improve some things and not others?
- Why do we have the skill to improve several activities, but tend to only make progress with a few and often only reach our potential with one?

By dividing learning into stages we can find some answers to these three questions. Benjamin Bloom called the stages of learning early, middle, and late. These stages parallel what Alfred North Whitehead referred to as the "Romance Stage," the "Precision Stage," and the "General Stage" in 1929.

Studies about human learning and development point out that what happens during the early or romance stages of development influences how long and how often individuals will continue to stay involved with an activity. The early or romance stage must be recognize for what it is. This stage is when the possibilities of continued engagement and the possibility of the improved subsequent skills exist. This is the stage when passion and a love of something can be nurtured. If we want people to fall in love with an activity then this awakening or arousing stage must be free of intimidation and frustration.

Studies show that without interest and passion there will be no love for playing a game or learning a subject. Without interest and love, the basic needs of human behavior and development are not being met, and this reality is often sidestepped when it comes to learning. Skill-development is a byproduct of free, self-motivated play. Pick-up games in parks and school yards, sports environments, and classrooms free of judgment and criticisms are all self-motivated play.

Studies also show that when the early or romance stage of development (the time to fall in love) is filled with required structured training, lots of instruction and competition, the freedom and enjoyment that can foster interest and passion for an activity are being suppressed. Over-managed, required, and structured instruction during the early or romance stage of development can cause individuals, young and old, to become frustrated and intimidated, thereby missing an opportunity to develop interest and passion for an activity and love of a game.

It is important to recognize that without the sense of pure enjoyment during the early stages of development, there will be a lack of lasting long-term interest. Without enjoyment and self-confidence during free play, there will be little opportunity to gain a feeling of self-worth and love of a game or subject during a journey of development. Human nature will find a place for a little structured training during the early or romance stage, as long as there is the opportunity to experience much more free play filled with exploration.

Suggestion: play for the pure sake of playing a game and you may develop a passion for and fall in love with that game, regardless of the score.

Studies show human beings engage in playful experiences all the time, without anyone telling them to do so. All humans chose to be playful, it is our nature! When it comes to sports, people of all ages stop playing, or play less frequently because:

- Practice is boring, drills when learning are of little value
- Emotional stress from excessive performance demands
- Negative coaching and feeling of failure
- Not enough free play or engagement

It seems imperative that before individuals fall in love with and become frequent participants in any activity, they must experience an introduction stage that Whitehead referred to as the Romance Stage.

"Man's thirst for survival in the future makes him incapable of living in the present."
Chang Tzv

Learning is a Personal, First Person Experience

"Does the approach to learning support efforts to think, apply, analyze, respond, develop, create, or invent? All of these are more valuable than simply knowing information. Application of information is the challenge for students and supporting that process with training, coaxing, scaffolding, and rethinking is the educators' challenge."
Leslie Richardson

Another hypothesis of this book is that approaches that aim to change unwanted outcomes are not as useful as approaches that enhance a student's learning potential. It is only after learning skills are enhanced that performance potential can improve. This insight merits serious attention! Learning to learn is an important first step.

Learning is emotional
Learning is drawing out
Learning is change
Learning is social

Learning is internal Learning is recognizing patterns and sequences
Learning is seeing options Learning is human development
Learning is mostly a non-conscious event
Learning is supported by past experiences Learning is a chemical process
Learning is supported by unworkable outcomes Learning is active, dynamic & organic
Learning is growth Learning is a synthesis of connecting
Learning is biological in nature Learning is self-regulation

Learning Potential

A well thought-out approach that is enhancing learning potential is also an approach to improving acts of learning.

When subject content is being shared by a brain-compatible information delivery system, a student's learning potential is normally enhanced and they learn faster and retain information and skills longer.

It is only after the learning potential is enhanced that performance potential can improve. Trying to change a poor habit or unwanted outcome will pay a lower return on the time and resources invested than improving a student's learning potential.

Learning potential is normally enhanced when students are given choices; they are using their self-discovery and self-assessment skills; or they are seeing unwanted outcomes as feedback for future reference in SMART, SAFE and PLAYFUL™ learning environments.

Marvin Minsky said, "Meaningful learning environments support where to look and how to look for information; they are not providing correct answers."

The Architecture of Learning

Highlights from the book *The Architecture of Learning: Designing Instruction for the Learning Brain,* by Kevin D. Washburn

Washburn states, "The term 'teacher' implies learning. If students do not learn, the teacher has been whistling in the wind." He went on, "Studies have shown that to be effective a teacher must align instruction methods with a learning cognitive process, the brain's way of constructing understanding and forming meanings."

Instruction design should be seen as different from lesson planning, a term traditionally used for pre-instruction preparation. Instruction design reaches beyond planning what content is going to be shared with the students. Designing takes into consideration a sequence of activities that are compatible with how the brain processes new information and emotions including:

Understanding students
Knowledge of the nature of learning
Awareness of subject matter

Combining these elements requires more than traditional lesson planning. It needs instruction design that mirrors the brain's connection to learning. Robert J. Marzano stated, "It is perhaps self-evident that more effective teachers use more effective instruction strategies." A teacher can know their topic, but are they aware of how to present the information so that it is compatible with how the brain seamlessly decodes, encodes, processes, and recalls information.

Washburn points out that the executives at Google say that the next big thing is "where everything will be connected – a connection that exists in a healthy brain." Within the human brain there is a network that connects everything. This is a behind-the-scene world of awareness and adjustments that supports the nature of learning.

Washburn's Five Elements of Learning

1. **Experience** – gives our brain raw data
2. **Comprehension** – allows the brain to sort, label, and organize sensory information
3. **Elaborating** – lets the brain examine information for patterns; recall prior experiences; and blend new and past experiences to construct understanding
4. **Application** – lets the brain use new knowledge
5. **Intention** – allows the brain to use new understanding in a wide range of contexts

The Design

The following are insights from Julie Dirksen, author of *Design for How People Learn.*

"The gap between where students are and where they would like to be can fall into the following areas:

- Knowledge gaps
- Skill gaps
- Motivation gaps
- Environmental gaps
- Communication gaps

What I can teach them is a different approach from what I can help them learn."

Benjamin Bloom's steps of learning were revised by Anderson and Krathowohl in 2001 as follows:

Recall goes to
      Understanding goes to
            Application goes to

Analysis goes to
Evaluate outcome goes to
Creating the next outcome.

Gloria Gery's (1991) steps of learning suggest we go from:
Familiarization, to
Comprehension, to
Conscious effort, to
Conscious action, to
Proficiency, to
Unconscious competence

Familiarization: Being able to recognize or recall principles and concepts.
Comprehension: Being able to explore concepts.
Conscious effort: Attempts to accomplish using a concept consciously.
Conscious action: Designing something using principles.
Proficiency: Successfully accomplishing things without laborious effort.
Unconscious proficiency: Using principles successfully without conscious thinking.

Dirkesen's suggestions included:
- Let individuals work out their own problems
- The teacher's job is to design games that make individuals feel smart
- Ask students what they know is a wrong answer
- Know what students are aware of and what they like
- Let students know what level of performance they should be working on
- Students frequently do not know what they do not know
- Give students access to what they need, then stop bothering them
- Reduce complexity of the environment
- Use metaphors or analogies
- All new learning is filtered through past experiences
- What can you do with learning styles? Not much; the evidence for the use of learning styles is weak

- A lot of learning gets encoded without lessons
- Have clear goals beyond correct answers
- Use action (doing) words in learning experiences
- Don't care if students cannot define it; see if they can *do* it
- Pay attention to key points in the objective outcome.

Some questions to pose to students are:

- Why are you learning this?
- How will learning this help you?
- What are the biggest challenges?
- What are some examples of your problems?
- What is the hardest thing for you to learn?
- What is the easy part?
- What could make it easier for you?
- What do you wish you knew when you first started?
- What does a typical example look like?
- What exception have you seen?
- How do you use the information?
- Can you tell me more about what you did?

NOTES:

_____
_____
_____
_____
_____
_____
_____
_____
_____
_____
_____
_____
_____
_____

Part Two

Counterintuitive Rethinking

- *Unwanted outcome when learning are "Desirable Developmental Difficulties"* - Harvard's Connecting the Mind Brain to Education Institute
- *"Ninety-nine percent of all learning is a non-conscious process."* Dr. Elaine Donchin
- *"People need to stop believing they have conscious control of their actions.'* David Brooks
- *"Introducing mistakes during training is important."* Robert Bjork
- *"Many broad facts about learning from years ago have been found to be no longer true."* Kurt Fischer

In the Know

It is often said that "smart people can know more than the rest of us" and that "having knowledge is power." It then follows that to be "in the know' is both useful and important.

So how does one get to be in the know? Answer = through meaningful learning.

When it comes to learning here are some elements to consider:

1. The information to be learned
2. How and where that information is being shared
3. How receivers of information are being asked to learn that information
4. The learner's past experiences

Note: Elements #2, #3 and #4 will influence whether meaningful learning is even possible.

That form follows function is a universally accepted principle. The *function* of approaches to learning is to give students the best opportunity (*form*) to gain and experience meaningful long-term learning and develop know-how skills.

"It's a miracle that the traditional methods of instruction have not entirely strangled all learning and curiosity of inquiry."
Albert Einstein

United States President Woodrow Wilson once said, "If you want to make enemies, try to change something." I am not trying to make enemies, but some approaches to learning do need to be rethought. When providers and receivers of information recognize that approaches to learning can be enhanced and modernized, that's the kind of ownership that can lead to a major transformation in education. When individuals have the tools to learn, better learning equates to better living.

I enjoy and benefit from my research about the brain's connection to learning systems, which I find useful in all learning environments. I find great pleasure in being exposed to some of the most respected and interesting minds in science and learning about the advances that science has made with regards to understanding the nature of learning. Tapping into perceptions about meaningful learning from leading research centers, universities and cognitive scientists provides us all with the opportunity to learn why both providers of information and receivers should be using brain-compatible information delivery systems.

The challenge, of course, is making approaches to education relevant for real world problem solving. In other words, what should individuals learn to enhance their reasoning and decision making skills, thereby becoming self-reliant? It is also a useful question to ask when individuals are not making progress in schools, colleges, business-training programs, or during sports instruction. Hopefully this book will help readers gain insights into that question; one that many believe is the eternal question.

Unfortunately, at the end of some lessons there are frustrated students who say, "You know what I learned today? I can't read," or "I can't do math," or "I can't play golf." Often students are only becoming aware of what's wrong and what they *can't* do. When approaches to learning are little more than a reaction to poor outcomes and not proactive, emotionally positive experiences, those approaches are not brain-compatible approaches for meaningful learning. A proactive experience develops self-confidence and self-assessment skills.

All healthy human beings come into the world as predisposed natural learners. Without consciously trying to learn, we just *can* and *do* learn (a survival skill). Unfortunately, when some students say 2+2=5 they are told they are wrong, instead of being asked how they arrived at that answer.

Tad James M.S., Ph.D said, "We use internal processing strategies for everything we do." All of our apparent external behaviors are controlled by internal processing strategies. *"It's what somebody does in their brain and nervous system that produces a result."*

Learning is Connecting

- The new with the Past
- Unwanted Outcomes with Inventing
- Words with Feelings
- Insight with what is Improvisation
- Thoughts with Images
- Self-regulation with Improving
- Perceptions with Realities
- Play with Progress
- Culture with Customs
- Environments with Safety
- Workable with Unworkable
- An Idea with Flexibility
- Self-image with Self-Reliance
- Physical with Mental
- Motion with Tempo
- Unconscious with the Present
- Neurons with Other Neurons

Our non-conscious mind is filled with information gained from past experiences, which we put to use on an as-needed basis. The brain recovers general patterns; relationships; and sequences that, if they make sense and have meaning, are stored in the non-conscious mind for future reference. Think of this sequence as a free download from a non-conscious mind filled with a wealth of possibilities available from the habits of the mind.

Eric Jensen, who wrote *Teaching with the Brain in Mind* in 1998, said that it was twenty years earlier that he was first introduced to the concept of the brain's connection to learning. On June 9, 1980, Jensen said he realized that Marshal Therver and other presenters at a learning seminar he attended clearly understood the value of using insights about the brain's connection to learning. As Mike Schmoker (author of *Voices*) said, *"The intellectual fitness of a healthy human brain should never be questioned."*

The research summarized here demonstrates the connection of the art of teaching to the science of learning. The brain does not do things badly, it does bad things competently. Students often experience a lack of progress through no fault of their own. **The hook to meaningful learning seems to be how information is presented to students.**

Individuals can learn a lot more than information in brain-compatible learning environments including: coping skills; accepting responsibility; self-discovery tools; intellectual and emotional confidence; approaches for internalizing; gaining insights for challenges; pride in what one is doing to grow; all while developing self-sufficiency.

Individuals grow into intellectual gym rats when guided by a brain-compatible information delivery system. "One of the marvelous things about the brain is that it is capable of taking over for us." [14] The process of learning is profoundly influenced by the culture of the environment in which that information is offered.

Brain-compatible approaches to learning key in on the process of learning, rather than the end product of right answers. Nature's plan for learning collaborates with real world environments, using approaches that could be called restless experimentation, which enlarges our imagination and expands our sense of the possibilities. Our brain chemistry either stimulates or suppresses all behavioral mechanisms, including learning. This process is based mostly on the context and culture of the approach to learning being used. We could say that brain-compatible approaches to learning are behavioral medicines.

Inconsistency is Valuable

While this may be a counterintuitive insight it is a reality:

---

[14] *Evolve Your Brain*, p. 255

Inconsistent outcomes are important keys to experiencing meaningful learning and developing to our full potential.

When you come across the term *"inconsistent"* does it give you a positive or negative feeling (emotion)? Our perception of inconsistency lays the foundation for experiencing meaningful learning. Before one makes their evaluation of inconsistency as positive or negative, they should keep in mind that nature, in all its wisdom, allows things to exist that help our survival – which inconsistency clearly does. When learning, we need the inconsistency of unwanted outcomes to reach our personal potential.

Most things human beings do are used as future reference points. Both wanted and unwanted outcomes have value for guiding our thoughts for future interactions with the environment.

"The mystery of life is not a problem to be solved, but a reality to be experienced."
Aart Van der Leeuw

It is useful to see things not as hard to do, but as things that can have inconsistent outcomes. For example, golf is not hard, it is inconsistent. The value of inconsistencies can be lost in a culture that processes unwanted outcomes as failures in need of fixing. This view has caused learning and progress to be less than they could have been.

In the business world the cost of money, volume of customers, and the number of sales are always inconsistent. This reality is accepted as a natural element of doing business and is used in positive ways to make conscious and unconscious adjustments for future business decisions. Learning environments should promote the same positive culture. Unfortunately schools and sports coaching tend to see inconsistency as a negative.

"How wonderful that we meet with a paradox; now we have some hope of making progress."
Neils Bohr

The suggestion here is that there is no failure, only usable feedback for future reference, based on the nature of inconsistency. By returning to what-to-do ideas (a positive emotion) and avoiding attempts to fix unwanted outcomes, meaningful learning is being supported. Unwanted outcomes are **"Desirable Developmental Difficulties,"** to use the words of Harvard's Connecting the Mind Brain to Education Institute. Studies show unwanted outcomes are four to five times more valuable for learning than workable outcomes, especially when seen as natural inconsistencies that we should learn from rather than try to fix.

When learning, if the natural elements of inconsistency are not seen for the tool they are meant to be, then growth, development and improving are all normally damaged. Mistakes are just information for future reference.

The natural events of evolution and natural selection were not, and are not today, aiming at perfection; their goal is function. The choices that nature was making in the past and still makes today are guided by the inconsistencies that exist in living and learning. This process is supporting functional outcomes on a journey of learning and developing; it is not trying for perfection. Living is at the core of learning, and learning is at the core of living.

Brain-compatible learning will become more attainable when inconsistent outcomes are seen as important components of meaningful learning. UCLA's Robert Bjork, the award winning scientist who researches the nature of learning, provided some eye opening insights in his paper – *How we Learn and Should Practice, Versus How we Think we Learn and*

F	**F**inds
A	**A**ccess
I	**I**nto
L	**L**earning,
U	**U**ncovering
R	**R**elevant
E	**E**xperiences

Should Practice. He wrote, "Paradoxically, certain conditions that promote forgetting and impair performance during instruction and practice, can actually enhance long-term retention and transfer." He went on "conversely conditions that retard forgetting and enhance performance during training, frequently fail to support long-term post-training retention and transfer."

Bjork said, "From a practical standpoint these findings point to reasons instructors are susceptible to using less effective conditions of instruction over more effective conditions (emphasizing poor outcomes). From a theoretical standpoint, such findings leave implications for the functional architecture of humans as learners".

Approaches to learning should focus on learning what-to-do, and avoid trying to fix unwanted outcomes or even mentioning them in a negative tone. Changing the cultural view of inconsistencies from unwanted outcomes to seeing them as a natural component of learning can accelerate learning. **Why do unwanted outcomes arrive? Because we are human!**

Bjork's studies suggest introducing mistakes and unwanted outcomes during training. Jack Nicklaus has said he deliberately performed mistakes during practice to help learn what to do when playing. Being exposed to unwanted events is more valuable than studying events, as principles outweigh rules.

Failure versus Feedback

Unfortunately, we are told to avoid failure. We are criticized for failure. We are told, *"Don't do that again."* We are afraid of failure — why?

One answer; we are programmed at some stage of our lives to see unwanted outcomes as failure. This view often prevents both providers and receivers of information from experiencing meaningful learning.

Realistically, unwanted outcomes are not an option; they always exist in the ever-changing environments that the real world presents. If you can accept that insight, your future choices are straight forward.

First, you can either continue to use an approach to learning that does not recognize what can be gained from experiencing unwanted outcomes, or you can see unwanted outcomes as valuable feedback for future references.

Approaches to brain-compatible learning have an appreciation for unwanted outcomes because of their transformative value. unwanted outcomes have the ability to become emotionally accepted for future reference (non-frustration) and not as failure, when we are learning with the brain in mind.

The steps and stages of meaningful learning often involve a counterintuitive approach in the direction of pushing previous boundaries, while not trying to fix or get something right.

Meaningful learning can be brought on by doing some rethinking about the value of unwanted outcomes. When unwanted outcomes are no longer seen as events to be negatively judged as failure and are recognized as important components of meaningful long-term learning, the approach to learning becomes more brain-compatible.

Errors Are Useful

"A man of genius makes no mistakes; his errors are validation and are the portals of discovery."
James Joyce

The brain-mind does many things well, but nothing perfectly. In their book, *Bozo Sapiens: Why to Err is Human*, researchers Michael and Ellen Kaplan offer many valuable insights into the nature of assumptions; predictions; doubt; error; and learning. What follows are some notes I made while reading their book with some of my own insights added.

The Kaplans pointed out that to err is human. Over time, humans had to adapt by testing assumptions and making predictions through trial and error. This process had the brain taking in information from workable and unworkable, wanted and unwanted outcomes, thereby re-wiring brain cell connections as an ongoing process.

Assumptions and predictions are more than important thinking tools; they are how a healthy brain functions. Human beings assume and predict our way through our daily lives. We are always harvesting information from our non-conscious minds, which is the underlying source of our learning, developing, and survival skills.

The same basic brain that we traveled out of caves with has been guiding the human race ever since. It was during the prehistoric times that our ancestors spent in caves, forests, and on savannas that the brain was being wired with many of our predestined assumptions which are found in the network of cell connections filled with prior knowledge.

We make assumptions all the time. We assume something will be good or bad. We assume and predict something will be interesting or not. We assume whether it is the right time to do something or not. We assume what will or will not work, etc.

Predictions and assumptions are the prisms through which we see life's choices and they come with errors that will be encoded in brain cells from which learning will come.

A healthy brain is efficient. It is filled with general just in-the-ball-park; detail-free concepts that provide short cuts and support learning. Studies show we actually could not function if we consciously knew all that was going on – hoping to avoid error.

Many useful ideas and thoughts resonate without detailed explanation. For example: the simple act of reaching out to open a door or a desk drawer was put into motion by a thought to do so (not an explanation). Now, if you were to write down or have to explain everything that took place when the door was being opened it would take a significant number of words to detail what occurred with the body, arm, hand, fingers, etc.

To know is to be allowed a choice. To choose includes choosing badly. Doubt and error are the start of wisdom in a world filled with false ideas. To use the Kaplan's words, "to find sense within non-sense, or meaning from meaningless, is the power of error."

There will always be more ways to err than to be valid. Studies show unwanted outcomes are more useful to learning than workable outcomes.

Volatility

To <u>Love Volatility</u> was a Wall Street Journal column[15] about the book *Antifragile: Things that Gain From Disorder.*[16] The book's author Nassim Nicholas Taleb is one of the foremost philosophers of our times; a trader and expert on probability.

Antifragility makes some suggestions to the business community that I feel approaches to learning could utilize.

In his book, Antifragile, Taleb refers to in his words "black swans." "In a world that is constantly throwing unexpected events our way (black swans), we must learn to benefit from disorder. He who is not antifragile will perish."

Taleb: "In economic life and in history, just about everything of some consequence comes from an unexpected event. Orderly events have little effect in the long-term because little is learned."

Taleb Suggests Five Rules

RULE 1: Think of the economy as being more like a cat than a machine.

Taleb: *"Cats find ways to take care of themselves; machines need someone to run and maintain them. The human body is wired with self-healing properties; machines are not. Mechanical systems must be precise in order to function; natural, healthy organic systems need some disorder to develop, such as a mind challenged to a new level."*

Nature of Learning: Brain-compatible approaches to learning accept unwanted outcomes as feedback for future reference, not as

---

[15] *Wall Street Journal*, Nov. 11, 2012, Matt Ridley's Mind and Matter Column
[16] Author Nassim Nicholas Taleb; Random House Publishing Group

something to be fixed. According to many studies "mistakes," unwanted outcomes, and disorder should be introduced when learning.

Taleb: *"Deprive your bones of stress and they will become brittle. Stifle and suppress natural fluctuations (inconsistency) makes for real problems because they cause variations, (which are important to learning) to be delayed and then become more damaging when they take place."*

RULE 2 – Favor business approaches that allow people to benefit from their own mistakes, not approaches where poor outcomes percolate into their system.

Taleb: *"Without failure in the restaurant industry, we would be eating cafeteria food. A tragedy can lead to examination and elimination of a cause of problems. Nothing fails in vain. Fragility should be seen for what it can be; beneficial to the collective enterprise of all business."*

Nature of Learning: Brain-compatible learning environments suggest students just do-it, observe it, and adjust-it if needed, based on past experiences (both wanted and unwanted.)

Taleb: *"Businesses that have learned to cooperate with volatility have a kind of growth similar to evaluation in the natural world, benefiting from the pressure of one error at a time, thereby becoming well functioning."*

RULE 3 – Small is beautiful, it is also effective.

Taleb: *"Size, when it exceeds a certain threshold, produces poor results."*

Nature of Learning: Too much information, too many details, going beyond core information has been shown to delay development.

RULE 4 – Trial and error beats out academic knowledge.

Taleb: "Tinkering (trial and error or playing with something without expectation) has typically played a larger role in progress than directed science when it comes to innovation and invention. Many great names, Charles Darwin, Henry Cavendish, William Parsons, and Rev. Thomas Baves were all known as hobbyists who were trial and error tinkerers, not academics and they outreached the model of driven science."

Taleb: "Many inventions were developed by practitioners in trial and error environments, drawing on a model of constant feedback from reality. Innovation does not require instruction; or what Taleb refers to as lecturing birds on how to fly."

Taleb: "There is an inverse relationship between the amount of formal education that a culture supports and the volume of trial and error training."

Nature of Learning: Trying to fix or get something right is not a brain-compatible approach to learning and changing. Adjustments that are guided by what-to-do insights are more valuable than following how-to directions.

RULE 5 – Decision makers must have skin in the game.

Taleb: "Romans forced bridge builders to sleep under a bridge after they completed building it. At no time in the history of human kind have there been more individuals in positions of power who do not take personal risk as an outcome of their actions. Managers of businesses that fail should have financial penalties."

Nature of Learning: When students are not making progress at a reasonable rate, the students normally do not need more education; the instructor or designer of the approach to learning being used needs more education.

Taleb: "Situations and things that experience volatility grow and improve under adversity, a crucial property of life in general. The dynamic process of volatility can be seen not just in business but also in the evolution of all things including our own existence on this planet."

Nature of Learning: The process of learning is clearly supported by volatility, as is the progress we make in our ever-changing real world environments.

<u>Look for function, not perfection</u>

<u>from the process of learning!</u>

It's a Process

The Mission Statement of this book was developed during a curious journey (which began in the late 1980s) about the nature of learning that I still pursue. It seems that effective learning is founded more on curiosity, imagination, self-discovery and self-evaluation than on how-to directions and corrections from a perceived expert. Try to open the minds of readers to all the possibilities revealed in the previous sentence. **"It is the process of learning, rather than subject content information, that strategies for teaching need to be aligned with." Catherine Twomey Fosnot.**

66

"If students do not understand the learning process (I would also add providers of information), the chief enzyme of education, they are not going to learn very much. To improve learning, teach students how to learn."[17]

In the fast paced, result-oriented culture that we live in today, some approaches to learning have become more of a business product, than the investment in students they are meant to be.

Terry Doyle states, "So few educators have had formal development in teaching practice."[18] Studies show that there would be less talk about poor schools, poor grades, poor sports skills and poor performing business approaches of if both teachers and students focused more on enhancing their approach to learning than on trying to fix unwanted outcomes.

In 1937, Heinz Werner drew our attention to the traditional emphasis on achievement (grades), rather than on the process of learning. He accurately predicted the unfortunate consequences of unprepared students for real world application of knowledge.[19] Then, in 1960, Jerome Bruner wrote *The Process of Education* which rivaled Alfred Whitehead's *The Aims of Education*. Both books highlighted the process of learning and the value of having individuals discover knowledge for themselves. What Werner, Bruner and Whitehead were sharing about learning in the past is now supported in the 21st century by current research. As Malcolm Knowles said, "Learning is more efficient using a learning plan than a course outline."

[17] *Redesigning Higher Education*, by Gardiner, 1994
[18] *Learning Centered Teaching*, by Terry Doyle and Todd Zakrajsek, p. 3
[19] *Fantasy and Feeling in Education*, by Richard M. Jones, p. 3

My Thoughts About "The Process"

"Get it wrong, then get it right, is the fundamental process in learning." **Doug Lemon**

Walk when you walk;
> **Talk when you talk;**
>> **Look when you look;**
>>> **Feel when you feel;**
>>>> **All without expectations and judgments in the process.**

- Freedom is not doing what you want; freedom is knowing who you are and simply and freely being in the process
- Intelligence is normally defined by behavior/behavior is influenced by predictions/predictions are influenced by past experiences and experience is what we use while in the process
- If you do not build it in the process, you will not understand it
- We are ourselves in the process, but results and outcomes are not who we are
- In the process outcomes are because of the process
- The process can be damaged when we are not ourselves
- In the process, we let go of emotions after unworkable outcomes
- Memories without negative judgments can be valuable to progress
- In the process we learn to let workable outcomes arrive – without avoiding unworkable outcomes
- In the process, learning happens somewhere between not knowing and knowing; between workable and unworkable.

- In the process we often do not know how we did it, but our unconscious does
- Stay in the process–no expectations about outcomes–no conscious thinking
- In the process, do not consciously add, subtract, or go from complex to simple
- Entering a learning environment can be a conscious act, but in the process, learning, more often than not, is an unconscious result
- Learning needs little else than to capture the reality that surrounds you in the process
- When learning, be who you are and stay in the process.
- In the process, the *self* in us is not a solid form; it is fluid, flexible, and portable
- In the process, the *self* in yourself is what meaningful learning and creativity travel through
- The process flows through a trust in your own mind, thoughts and feelings
- When you go deep enough into the process, it will take the *self* in you where you need to go
- Deep can't be found in the width of details, deep exists in personal insights uncovered in the process
- The process has no straight lines; its strength is found in randomness that lacks a map, while supporting self-reliance
- In the process there is no wrong or right way. All approaches are useful some of the time
- In the process the creator is separated from the conscious editor. The creator in the process is free to explore and experience unconsciously
- The process does not focus on the power of the conscious editors by hearing their empty words of how-to directions and details

- In process, your own mind is all you have, so let it work unconsciously
- The mind is where our first impressions and thoughts are born as choices made unconsciously in the process
- The mind unconsciously remembers and so do you in the process
- When the scared or insecure leave, suddenly unintended, raw energy arrives in the process
- In the process, inspiration means taking in what actually is happening or being felt
- In the process no one is broken or in need of fixing; they are on a journey of development
- Working with a beginner's mind set every day, at all skill levels, is an opportunity to start where one should always start, in the process
- The beginner's mind is a gift from the process
- In the process, working as beginner is something to anticipate.
- In the process, it is fair to say a healthy brain is always operating on our behalf
- Within the process, we are adjusting to the environment, even though we are unaware of these internal changes.
- Never tire of helping others to become aware of the process
- In the process learning is always alive with possibilities, not with answers

Hardwired

A *Harvard Business Review* article by Nigel Nicholson titled, How hardwired is human behavior? contains insights about our homo sapiens species. Many of our early ancestors' survival traits dating back 200,000+ years ago to the African savannah are still hardwired into our 21st century brains. This article has many insights and suggestions that are based on brain-compatible information delivery systems. Some aspects of human behavior, including the skill of non-conscious learning, are biologically inborn and universal. Nicholson used six sources of scientific research to uncover the influence of these hard wired traits (Anthropology; Behavioral Genets; Neuropsychology; Paleontology; Social Psychology).

Hardwired: People are hardwired to use emotions as their first filter of all the information they receive.

Learning Approach: Avoid criticism; judgments; negative evaluations of unwanted outcomes.

Hardwired: People are hardwired to avoid taking risks when feeling relatively secure and fight when feeling threatened.

Learning Approach: People will act and think creatively when given support in a safe space.

Hardwired: People are hardwired to feel more self-confident than is really justified.

Learning Approach: Help people to realistically evaluate the situation and challenges they face.

Hardwired: People are hardwired to quickly classify situations, people and experiences into good-bad categories.

Learning Approach: Promote the value of objective evaluation. Something is what it is; not good or bad, easy or hard.

Hardwired: People are hardwired to participate for status and ego.

Learning Approach: Encourage the engagement of the task for the sake of the task itself.

Hardwired: People are hardwired so that hearing positive remarks does not undo the damage of negative remarks.

Learning Approach: Always be proactive; stay away from negative remarks.

Hardwired: People are hardwired to seek excellence.
Learning Approach: Promoting the recognition of excellence is the result of a journey, not a healthy destination.

Goals

Having goals is useful when learning. There are **outcome goals** that focus on getting to an end result (i.e.: I want to accomplish this or that). There are also **process goals** that are made up of tools (mental, emotional, and physical) used for supporting acts of reaching one's potential. What process (approach) will be used to reach one's potential, is a question that should be addressed when learning and performing. What is your recipe for learning?

When process goals receive more attention than outcome goals, the journey of reaching one's potential is less frustrating and more efficient. The reverse is true when outcome goals travel into our conscious thoughts, progress becomes difficult.

When individuals stay in the process of doing, and accepting results without judgments, workable outcomes are accomplished non-consciously, or more efficiently. Brain-compatible information delivery systems can create the kind of safety net that helps individuals avoid the frustrations that normally accompany consciously focusing on the culture of outcome goals when learning or performing.

As Jack Petrash, author of Understanding Waldorf Education Teaching from the Inside – Out said, "Rather than focusing educational work solely around the object of acquiring knowledge, creating a meaningful learning process becomes the focus." I have learned from respected research that many traditional assumptions about teaching and learning are more myth than valid.

Approaches to meaningful learning have process goals that are free of value judgments.

NOTES:

Part

Three

Lower Frustration

&

Intimidation

"The relationship between provider and receiver of information must be caring, equitable and responsive. It must be firm and safe"
Matthew H. Bowken, Ph.D, MA

The nature of learning requires being comfortable with being uncomfortable during the process of change.

Nurturing Words

"All that we are is the result of what we have thought. The mind is everything. What we think, we become."
Mahesh Yogi

"Words are powerful performance enhancing drugs," David Alred. What we say, how we say it, and when we say it can enhance performance.

Often it is an overlooked reality that words can be destructive. Words and the manner in which they are being shared can inflict damaging emotions, including self-doubt. But, by examining how we respond and communicate, we can become more skilled with the use of words.

When it comes to helping someone learn or improve simply having subject knowledge is insufficient. A skilled use of words is needed by both teachers and students. Use guiding words, not criticisms or judgments when sharing content. Guidance uncovers possible solutions by providing information that inspires new insights. Guidance avoids trying to fix poor habits or reacting to unwanted outcomes.

"Everyone has the right to feel safe in learning environments. Individuals cannot do what they are capable of, or be who they are, if they are afraid. It is a nurturing force, not judgments and criticisms that support lifelong learning."[20]

Becoming an advocate for students requires gaining some accurate insights about the nature of learning. Efficient learning environments offer words of consideration and guidance, not criticism and corrections. Rosabeth Moss Kanter, a Harvard Business School Professor, author of sixteen books said, "Confidence, a belief that the outcome of our efforts will be positive, is nurtured by others. Educators (or any providers of information) and students should pay attention to what is good, not what is bad. Look for

---

[20] *The Art and Science of Teaching*, p.28

small wins that will support bigger success later on. Look for milestones to move on from later."[21]

Mark Twain wrote, **"Really great people make you feel that you too, can become great."** To draw out what individuals are capable of is the aim of efficient brain-compatible learn-and-develop environments, with students being given that old "I can do it" feeling.

Brain-compatible approaches are more a process of "outstruction," than instruction (they draw out and use what is there) in order to support new learning based on a student's past experiences. Helping someone to learn and improve is a series of events often filled with conflicts that call for a response. Now, think about the learning environments and ask yourself why words from teachers have consequences that can support or suppress learning. What is the difference?

A Presentation

The following is from my opening remarks at the 2012 World Golf Fitness Summit.

"The aim of this presentation is to cause lots of curiosity about combining the "art of teaching" with the "science of learning." That said how do we actually go from not knowing to knowing?

The words we use are powerful. The emotional damage done by a negative remark cannot be undone by positive statement. There are words that support acts of learning while other words suppress it. The power of conversation influences how we do or do not learn; how we grow or do not grow as a person; how we spread useful ideas or not.

---

[21] *New York Times* article September 19, 2004

Thoughts, words and conversation are at the heart of everything we do, including learning. When we are transferring information we use words. Hopefully the words we use are compatible with how the brain best learns.

How Do We Support Meaningful Learning?

Take Risks.

Don't Fix Anything!

Take Emotions Into Consideration.

Take Past experiences into Consideration.

Make Students Feel Smart and Safe.

Join the Art of Learning with the Science of Learning.

When frustration and intimidation are removed from acts of learning, clever, creative, competent students with the tools to adjust and cooperate with ever-changing environments emerge. Our fight or flight instincts were probably not as important to our evolution as the skills of cooperation.

Avoiding damaging words, frustration and intimidation can move approaches to learning beyond the culture and customs of many traditional teach-to-fix approaches to learning. When providers of information want students to experience meaningful learning they should make them feel smart, while developing self-reliance tools. Eliminating intimidation and frustration is one of the aims of these approaches to learning."

Insights

Matthew H. Bowker, Ph.D MA, a researcher who explores critical thinking stated, "The relationship between the provider and the receiver of information must be caring, equitable and responsive. It must be firm and safe. The tone must be playful and creative so students can think, converse, listen and question without feeling either lost or crushed."

"Creating an educational environment in which pleasure, stimulation, and challenge flourish is an important mission. Also, students are more likely to learn, remember, and make subsequent use of those experiences with respect to which they had strong, positive emotional reactions. It has become evident that any portrait of human nature that ignores motivation and emotion proves to be of limited use in facilitating human learning."

Cognitivists have proposed various models of how emotions can structure, guide, and influence mental representations. **These models point to a simple truth: "if one wants something to be attended to, mastered, and subsequently used, one must be sure to wrap it in a context and words that engage the positive emotions.** Conversely, experiences devoid of positive emotional impact are likely to be weakly engaging and soon forgotten leaving nary a mental representation behind." [22]

The culture of brain-compatible approaches to learning supports the development of self-reliant individuals. I assume every parent, educator, employer and sports coach wants the result of their efforts to be self-reliant individuals. Brain-compatible approaches to learning support achieving that result.

Students need to be free from the pressure to secure approval. Labeling is disabling. When teachers and students are negatively evaluating and not accepting unwanted outcomes as feedback for future reference, they can cause anxiety and resistance.

Emotionally compatible approaches to learning acknowledge the effort to make progress and do not focus on the outcome, be it workable or unworkable. Telling someone "you were great," is not as helpful as acknowledging their effort in learning environments.

---

[22]*The Disciplined Mind,* by Howard Gardner, p. 77

"Praise can be punishment," (Alfie Kohn). In psychotherapy, judgmental and evaluating praise is avoided. State what you like, using a realistic picture of accomplishment, not judgmental praise. Individuals benefit more from specific information and appreciation of effort, than hearing they are good. For example, *"Good job, you stayed positive during the lesson."*

Students should be presented with several situations in which they can make choices. Providing options for students supports learning and improvement. Unfortunately, students learn what they have lived with. Many students have learned to doubt their own judgments, to doubt their own abilities and to distrust their own intentions when teachers are unskilled at using words. When students believe they can learn, they will stay engaged and be interested in observing, experimenting, improvising, inventing and developing an information base that is personal in nature.

Dr. Haim Ginott said, "Many teaching problems will be solved in the next few decades. There will be new learning environments and new means of instruction. One function however will always remain with the teacher: to create the emotional climate for learning. No machine, sophisticated as it may be, can do this job." Dr. Ginott went on to say, "I have come to a frightening conclusion. As a teacher, I am the decisive element in the classroom. It is my personal approach that creates the climate. It is my daily mood that makes the weather. I possess tremendous power to make a student's life miserable or joyous. I can be a tool of torture or an instrument of inspiration. I can humiliate or humor, hurt or heal. In all situations it is my response that decides whether a crisis will be escalated or deescalated, and a student humanized or dehumanized."

How do students get inspired? Approaches to progress with a culture that makes individuals feel smart inspire and enhance self-esteem as they develop their solutions for the task at hand. I believe that making students feel smart is the main responsibility of an educator, parent, employer, or sports coach.

Trying to learn in a state of anxiety that is concerned about results can fragment progress. The energy that is spent to protect our self-image from anxiety could be used for making progress. When learners are protecting themselves (nature's plan for survival when we are in danger) from criticisms and corrections, they cannot experience a journey that leads to meaningful learning. The wisdom of necessity has wired human beings to interact and move toward what is interesting and lacks danger. We learn by having a full sensory experience with objects in environments that are not seen as threats.

Nature has biologically wired man's intelligence and the wisdom of his intuition to consider the implications of our actions. When learning environments are filled with criticisms and corrections they become a threat and nature's protection system considers the implications and automatically closes down man's natural "instincts" to do, observe and adjust. Studies show that under stress some neural pathways actually close down, making learning more difficult.

It may help to see the brain as having information and the mind as filled with emotions that are learned after birth, influencing our ability to learn more information. Research from cognitive science and other disciplines shows that the nature of learning is influenced by the brain's limbic or emotional system as information travels through the SELF found in self-discovery, self-organization, self-assessment and self-confidence, to name a few of mankind's many "self" skills. New learning is encoded while physical and emotional safeties are also being evaluated. Brain-compatible information delivery systems do not create the kind of stress that has a negative influence on emotions. Learning is mostly an emotional event, and brain-compatible learning approaches take this reality into consideration.

What unifying learning experience can meet the needs of all the diverse segments of our society?

What supports the kind of learning that transforms information from its source (books, magazines, teachers, etc.) into knowledge for use in real world environments?

Answer = brain-compatible information delivery system.

Emotions

"The greatest discovery of my generation is that a human being can alter his life by altering his activities."
William James

I find it interesting that many books about the brain's connection to learning begin by discussing the interplay between emotions and our cognitive capabilities. The reality is that emotions can help or hinder acts of learning. In the center of our brain lies the limbic system; this is called the emotional brain. Richard J. Davidson, Ph.D pointed out that the pre-frontal cortex of the brain is also involved in emotions in his must read book, *The Emotional Life of Your Brain*, written with Sharon Begley.

Emotions are influenced by chemicals that are released throughout our body as we interact with our environment. Some chemicals support, whereas other chemicals suppress meaningful learning. Unfortunately, because of the strong influence emotions have on learning, people of all ages tend to hear bad news first and loudest. Information providers should not assume that they can balance or off-set negative messages with positive messages.

Telling someone they have failed is perhaps the most discouraging and potentially dangerous message there is. It should be recognized that emotions can never be fully suppressed and that is why providing meaningful feedback should not be about what was wrong.

Managing emotions in learning and performing environments is one of the keys to being an efficient learner or teacher.

Emotions can influence:

- self-regulation
- attention seeing options
- problem solving skills
- memory
- heart rate
- learning potential

It has been found that cognitive performance suffers in environments that have excessive stress, fear, or social judgments. These environments compromise the neural process of emotional regulation, causing the brain to go into a protective mode, closing down some of our neural pathways.

One of the brain's natural tools is self-protection, which can reduce the number of neural pathways available for learning when we are under excessive stress. Learning becomes less efficient with fewer neural pathways available throughout the brain under excessive stress.

The negative side effect of fewer neural pathways available throughout the brain include: depression, confusion, reduced concentration, less efficient vision, poor spatial thinking, and poor working memory. Because learning involves an emotional experience, struggling with difficulties can be emotionally painful, damaging acts of learning, when individuals do not fully accept difficulties as valuable feedback for future reference – struggling supports learning.

Studies at Columbia University Teacher's College and Harvard University's Graduate School of Education have shown that the design and structure of "the approach" to learning that individuals experience will influence their future employment opportunities, living conditions, physical and mental well-being and their pace of progress in sports and other endeavors. Meaningful learning can seem magical, but it is not magic, it has to do with the brain's connection to the approach being used.

Often we do not know what we need to know, until we are shown. I would learn that how providers and receivers of information interact with each other could overcome adversity, transforming acts of learning into a proactive positive experience by moving beyond negative reactions to unwanted outcomes.

I would learn that when it comes to learning, subject content s not the challenge. How approaches to learning are organized is the challenge. I would learn that the cultures of efficient, approaches to learning were formed with the brain in mind.

The culture and customs of some approaches to learning can carry a message that supports learning, and other approaches put forward a message that is counterproductive, suppressing long-term recall of information and skills. Studies show our capacity to recall information is much smaller than our brain's seemingly limitless capacity to encode information. **Therefore it is import ant that approaches to learning enhance the ability to understand and recall information.** I would also learn that memory is more an act of rebuilding than recalling.

Individuals are less educated about a topic at the start of a journey of learning than they will be as that journey continues. That said; keep in mind studies show that people who are less educated about a topic are less likely to process stress forming complex information.

Emotions are chemicals. We could say we do not like something; we like or love the chemicals that are released because of that something. Every cell has an emotional component. Everything, including learning, starts in our cells and the chemical exchanges in which they are involved.

Words and Thoughts

Break a cycle of poor learning by using the brain in an optimal fashion.

The brain is involved in everything we do. This includes the processes of learning, thinking, feeling, acting, and how we personally perceive and choose to go about doing things. How we get along with others and every decision we make or do not make are also brain based. This internal process is influenced by the kind of chemicals released into the brain and nervous system, which is mostly influenced by the type of words we use and the thoughts we have leading up to and during our interactions.

The kind of chemicals released (depending on the type of words we use) will either emotionally support or suppress what we are trying to accomplish. We could say that information is being transferred to an individual's emotional memory, not to the individual itself. Information and skills that we have acquired exist in the form of brain cell chemical information. These cells of information form connections to other cells creating our long term memory and guide posts for future reference.

As we take in new information this creates more cell connections in the brain, a mostly non-conscious process that is comparing new information with prior knowledge. This process includes an evaluation of new information to find out if the information makes sense and has any meaning to us based on our past experiences (again mostly non-conscious). When information makes sense and has meaning it will move on from a very short stay in our working memory into our long-term memory. Approaches to learning that use stories and metaphors support the transfer of information and enhance long-term memory. Both the brain and emotional self-love stories that connect new and prior experiences.

When new information does not make sense or has no meaning, it is discarded as not useful for future reference (survival). Only a very small percentage of the new information the brain takes in will reach long-term memory. Studies show that of the four million bits of information the brain takes in per second it only retains about two thousand bits.

REALITY: One brain cell can be connected to over one million other cells out of the trillions of cells that exist in the brain. This network of connected brain cells forms a brain information highway that brain cells use to send information to each other (a survival skill).

Within the brain, learning or problem solving is a team effort of cooperation among brain cells based on past experiences. We often read about a fight or flee response that humans have, but it was acts of cooperation that supported the survival of the human race. We learned to cooperate with who and what was in our ever changing environment during our journey into the 21st century. What we humans do as we interact with our surroundings is based on a group decision from many different sources of information (cells) within the brain and body. This mostly non-conscious cooperation process is a predisposed skill that we come into the world with at birth.

During any of the many decisions that the brain is making every mil a second, the cells in the brain act like a large committee, with most of its members talking at the same time. This process has brain cells simultaneously exchange information and create options and answers for all the split second problems being solved in our real world ever changing environments.

One cell may have one kind of information (size), another cell may have different information (speed), another cell may have information about (safety) and so on, with any answer or outcome a blend of new and old information from many different cells (acts of cooperation). Again, keep in mind this process is influenced by how the brain has wired its cells into a network or pattern, influenced by the entire nervous system, which in influenced by our thoughts, words and emotions about the situation at hand.

Joe Dispenza, D.C., author of *EVOLVE Your BRAIN*, who was also featured in the hit movie "What the Bleep Do We Know," points out that all humans with healthy brains want to be good accomplishers. We want to do things done well. He suggests that a useful view of the brain is that the brain is filled with possibilities and our observations (physical and emotional) move forward based mostly on unconscious emotional choices based on all the possibilities that are encoded in the brain.

These ranges of possibilities are formed from the data we have encoded in the brain over time. The kind of words and thoughts an individual hears or uses to evaluate and describe the information the brain is taking in creates an emotional influence, (negative or positive) on the outcome of what is possible. Some of the words that could be attached to past experiences when they took place include; good, bad, safe, unsafe, hard, easy, can do, can't do, I like, I don't like, all of which influence future possibilities.

Everything we have done in the past including our motions, our thoughts, what we have learned, our wanted and unwanted outcomes, all come together emotionally to unconsciously formed a list of possibilities that we can use or not use to be good accomplishers. Again, this emotional learning process is influenced by the words and thoughts (negative and positive) that we use when we are engaged in acts of accomplishing. During acts of learning the brain is evaluating physical safety, the emotional climate and new information all at the same time.

REALITY: It's the story we tell our self and the kind of words we use that cause the release of the kind of emotional chemicals that will either support or suppress our ability to be good accomplishers.

Warning! Negative words, thoughts and stories produce results below our potential.

Words are the most powerful performance enhancing drug when used in a brain compatible way, but when they are not compatible they become a most powerful performance suppressing drug.

REALITY: Learning is an experience. All experiences are emotional. The brain is the gateway to learning on a path of emotional experiences.

The implications are that when learning the brain is influenced by emotions that for the most part are based on past experiences. Fear hinders being a good accomplisher. When learning, emotionally safe and supportive environments that are free of judgment support meaningful learning and good accomplishments. The transfer of information should be aimed at the internal emotional self not at the external self of individuals.

All systems in the brain can learn implicitly and unconsciously based on past experience. Implicit non-conscious learning is a human being's main form of learning. Consciously recognizing that implicit, non-conscious learning exists supports long-term learning. Implicit learning involves using information that is personal to individuals to learn and self-discover with. Implicit learning is learning for the pleasure of learning. On the other hand explicit learning has an external reward in mind and is mostly founded on information from a teacher. Studies show that explicit approaches to learning are not as useful as self-regulated implicit approaches.

It is fair to say that learning and most everything we do is based on how the brain is wiring itself from second to second. Based on the way it is wired at that second the brain goes into action internally *before* any external action occurs. External actions are a response to the brain's internal emotional interpretation of the external world at that second (safe, unsafe, good, bad, hard, easy). Meaningful approaches to learning are speaking to the internal, emotional self of individuals. How we talk to ourselves and the words others use when we are learning have a profound influence on being good accomplishers. Our personal perceptions, based on prior experiences, are responsible for how the brain is wired at the start of our interactions with the ever changing environment.

For example, when we pick up a jar to twist the top off the brain makes predictions about how much strength is needed to accomplish this task. This prediction is based on prior experiences and how the brain wired itself based on those experiences.

Now the genius of the human brain takes center stage! If untwisting the top takes more muscle power than first used the inter-connected volume of information in our brain's cells comes up with a trial and error adjustment – different way to go about the task in a mil a second. This may include holding the jar at a different angle, placing the fingers differently, the use of more muscles may be called into action, etc., each of which are non-conscious choices that come from our memory of all prior experiences, not just other attempts at opening jars. We automatically and unconsciously come up with an adjustment to our attempts until the task is successful or abandoned.

The brain's connection to learning is influenced by the reality that the words we and others use (positive or negative) are at the foundation of the internal thoughts that always arrive before we act. This internal message board is either helping or hurting individuals perform up to their potential. Gearing approaches to learning in the direction of thoughts and words that cooperate with releasing positive emotion chemicals supports the nature of meaningful learning.

When it comes to acts of learning, using non-traditional 21st century approaches for traditional problems joins the art of teaching with the science of learning. Trial and error adjustments are the tools of the nature of learning. Errors and struggling are valuable components not to be seen as failure, but as important feedback for future conscious and non-conscious reference points.

Words are the most powerful influence on performance outcome!

WORDS

- Words create or suppress interest
- They cause every kind of emotion
- They build or destroy confidence
- They construct thoughts and answers
- They describe impressions and insights
- They are true of false
- They can be warm or cold
- They hurt or support
- They are on time or to late
- They are long or short
- They proactive or reactive
- They are ours or someone else's
- They are deep or shallow
- They are meaningful or not
- They are remembered or forgotten
- They help or do not
- They make sense or create confusion
- They are joyful or sad
- They are polite or rude
- They are to the point or evasive
- They are important or not
- They can cause creativity and growth or suppress it
- They can be constructive or destructive

Consider making a list of words you may want to rethink.

_____

_____

_____

_____

_____

_____

_____

_____

_____

_____

_____

_____

_____

_____

_____

_____

_____

_____

_____

_____

_____

_____

_____

_____

_____

_____

_____

_____

_____

Part Four

Insights

"The strongest principle of growth lies in human choice."
George Elliot

Everyone believes that learning is a good thing, but most of us
know so little about it. To support meaningful learning we
need to be aware of where it comes from.

The Value of Questions

"Did you ask any good questions today?" - Evelyn W. Deluty

In the 2010 fall issue of *Thought and Action*, a National Education Association Journal, and several educators discussed the topic of learning. Matthew H. Bowker and Evelyn Wortsman Deluty talked about the value of students asking questions. How to help students learn was discussed by Robert Zemsky and Lisa A. Sheldon. Research that can be demonstrated objectively in the concrete factual value of reality was discussed by Joyce Lucas-Clark. Thomas Axter talked about the future of education and Kristen Dierking talked about keeping approaches to learning interesting. What follows is my short summary of one hundred and sixty pages of their thoughts on learning.

"Did you ask a good question today?" is what Evelyn W. Deluty said that Nobel prize winner Isidor Isaac Rabi's mother would ask every day after school, instead of, *"what did you learn in school today?"* Perhaps there are no poor questions, but some are much more valuable than others. Questions are curious thoughts; the kind of thinking that promotes intelligence in growing the brain through answers.

Rabi's mother indirectly initiated him to the habit of inquiry; she understood that the roots of all learning are circulated by a mindset that emphasizes the active process of questioning rather than the passive gathering of facts.

Matthew H. Bowker pointed out that in the past we have focused on how teachers should ask questions and how students answered them, overlooking the value of helping individuals develop their own questioning skills when learning. Bowker said if teachers are always ready to ask a provocative question, their students do not have the need to take on that responsibility.

Bowker noted that several studies have shown that individuals demonstrate greater thought, complexity, initiative and personal engagement when teachers do not ask questions, but instead state propositions or offer non-question alternatives.[23]

Joyce Lucas-Clark pointed out **that presenting facts or answers without developing questions produces the kind of environment in which everything is already settled.** The primary objective of meaningful learning, according to Clark, is to improve students' ability to ask insightful questions, using answers as stepping-stones from question to question.

Bowker wrote that in Marshall McLuhan's view when the teacher is the one who constructs the most interesting questions, problems, or critical challenges, students become dependent upon the teacher to create inquiry. On the other hand, a question-centered approach that is based on students' questions develops students who engage in course material as independent thinkers.

According to Bowker, requiring students to create their own questions helps them understand how answers are connected and beg for additional questions. In this environment, the questions themselves are the answers.

Bowker – the important value of asking questions is in the ability to abstract from things, to unlock their meanings, courses, and consequences.

Bowker – Questioning involves speculating about possibilities both real and unreal, given and hypothetical, which is an immensely creative act. Questioning requires that the object not be seen just as it is.

Bowker – Questions probe to find something that is not already recognized, thereby discovering relationships and possibilities that are not yet given.

---

[23] *Practice of Questioning,* by Dillon

Bowker – In learning environments, questions must be keeping pace with answers. Both questions and answers must be appropriate to the levels of experience and cognitive development and functioning.

Bowker – Some believe that the purpose of education is to store up definitive answers in one's mind, but this does not promote the development of reasoning and deductive skills that create flexible knowledge and portable thinking.

Bowker said McLuhan pointed **out that our capacity to generate answers is often less important than our ability to question answers we already have**.

Bowker – Many providers of information aspire to a state that a problem received a perfect answer, which is actually not conducive to the development of a creative mind. It deprives individuals of the need to explore on their own, as they question more independently, revising answers.

Bowker – The relationship between the provider and receiver of information must be caring, equitable, and responsive. It must be firm and safe. The tone must be playful and creative so students can think, converse, listen and question without feeling either lost or crushed.

Deluty – **pointed out that inquiry is the pivotal skill in the demonstrative process of meaningful learning.** It's trying to judge for oneself rather than simply learning facts. Asking questions can transform ones' mind from a passive recipient to an active participant in the process of deliberation and learning.

Bowker – **Often there is a problem with a Socratic based approach to learning when the teacher takes control of most of or all the inquiry.**

Bowker – The teacher who stays on top of students, one who is always the questioner, one who squeezes work out of the students, may produce students who have stored up the material, but not students who are critically learning. "One can only judge critically through practice" *The Life of the Mind, Part One, Thinking*, by Bowker (p. 215).

Deluty – **Learning to judge for oneself takes place when the act of transmission is not merely intended to import facts, but rather to awaken students' questions.**

Deluty – In his book, *Goal Teaching – matter of living the mystery*, Parker Palmer talked about questions that demonstrated the students' ability to think critically and judge for themselves.

Deluty – There can be an interaction process that emerges between the knower and the known. When this is applied to teaching and learning the results shy away from a fixation on the content of curriculum and instead are intended to draw students into the process. **Palmer recognized that learning starts when individuals reflect critically, not when they are forced to remember facts.**

Deluty – When approaches to learning evolve through questions from students, students are called upon to tap into their inner (nonconscious) resources and become participants in the process of learning rather than just bystanders.

Deluty – Questioning helps students leap across the gap that separates passive learning from animated participation in the transmission of knowledge. **Questions are a sure sign that individuals are thinking critically.**

Deluty – The mere assemblage of facts, no matter how great, is of no worth, without the habit of reflective inquiry to judge them.

Deluty – the ability to ask a reflective question is the root of all change and progress.

This issue of *Thoughts and Actions* also included ideas about learning from L. Sheldon. When Sheldon talked about motivation, she said her goal, as a teacher was to facilitate student learning, promote goal attachment and encourage academic momentum. Sheldon pointed to the value of intrinsic motivation. She said, **"What separates successful students from the less successful is their ability to navigate obstacles and maintain motivation towards their goals."** Getting derailed is a common problem.

The essence of motivation, she felt was found in these two acronyms:

OARS – **O**pen-ended questions, **A**ffirmations, **R**eflective listening, **S**ummary statements

FRAMES – **F**eedback, **R**esponsibility, **A**dvice, **M**enu, **E**mpathy, **S**elf-efficiency

Oars

Open-ended questions cannot be answered with "yes" or "no." They allow students to tell their story.

Affirmation – morale boosting statements that help build confidence and feelings of improvement in their students.

Reflective listening – listening and understanding what students say without judgment.

Summary – for students, it is a chance to provide additional information and also be a reminder of action that needs to be taken. In my experience, keeping students curios keeps them motivated.

Frames

Feedback – a clear, non-judgmental way that articulates the current behavior and the goal of new behavior.

Responsibility – Behavior is owned by the students, and therefore it is up to them to change it if they need to.

Advice – provide new perspectives or options to consider, it must be the student's choice.

Menus – offer more than one selection to a problem and allow the student to choose.

Empathy – acknowledge that change can take time and work.

Self-efficiency – express a belief that the student has the potential to be successful increases the feeling of improvement in students.

Motivational conversation places responsibility for change and success in the hands of the student. Avoid confronting change head on, as this only feeds resistance, which then becomes the root of the problem, and not the behavior itself.

Barbara Fischer said **to avoid seeing students as consumers to give something to and help them gain something.** Create environments and have ideas mingle and give rise to new knowledge (know-how skills). Develop environments where more is being heard than is being said.

When Joyce Lucas-Clark talked about science, she said it appeals to human emotions and is characterized by enhancing uncertainty. Science is supported by gathering information and experimentation (sounds like how we learn anything). Randall E. Jedule said **"When I learned about active learning, it was as if the goddess of education waved a magic wand and turned me in a new direction.** I devoted my doctoral research to how teaching might be altered through cooperation."

Thomas Anixter expressed concerns that approaches to education are taking on business's focus to maximize profit.

Kristen Dierking stated approaches to education must move beyond simply feeding facts to students without asking them to think creatively or critically about the material. "I didn't want to just dish out information; I wanted to provide content in a way that would help students retain material. I began to use real life examples when appropriate to illustrate concepts as clearly as possible. I often found that once you agree on a viewpoint, you're likely to forget it. I try to have students debate their point of view."

"I want students to incorporate what they learn into the body of knowledge that they can carry with them, thinking in a diverse manner. I spend considerable time encouraging students to examine why they think what they think. Asking students to say or write something organized has produced many new insights and comments. It helps to know the concept behind a student's organized work."

"I encourage creative risk taking. I emphasize how important creative work is and how necessary their kind of thinking would be in the student's future lives. Building a student's confidence in his or her ability to innovate is invaluable. I try to help students to see the world in a way they had never previously considered."

Learning and Innovation

Creating Innovation by Tony Wagner, has been called a ground breaking book and what I believe is a must read for anyone who has an interest in the topic of learning. Tony Wagner is an Education Fellow at Harvard's Technology and Entrepreneurship Center, who researched what supports and what suppresses innovation and learning. Wagner conducted over 150 interviews with students and their parents; teachers and professors; engineers and scientists; artists and musicians; entrepreneurs and corporate C.E.Os.; military leaders and public officials for this book. His interviewees span such a wide range of career backgrounds it is my impression that he heard more common denominators than differences. These insights also revealed brain-compatible approaches to learning. Some of Wagner's findings and impressions include the following:

When it comes to the topics of innovation and learning many studies and respected research reveal that the United States is falling behind the rest of the world. The Information Technology and Innovation Foundation states, "the United States has made the least progress of the forty (40) nations studied in regards to improving innovation capacity over the last decade." The 2010 *Bloomberg Business Week* annual rankings of the most innovative companies noted that, "the majority of corporations in the top twenty-five (25) ratings are based outside the United States."

The film, The Finland Phenomenon: Inside the World's Most Surprising School System points out that when comparing similar realities about education systems, the United States is not achieving the successful results some of the other nations are experiencing. Every year in the United States there are many examples of meaningful learning and innovation taking place, but less than in the past. What is being side-stepped and overlooked when it comes to supporting innovation and learning? The following are some of the answers Wagner received when he asked the interviewees to define "innovation."

"I do not define it technically because it is an art. Innovation is about the process by which new things take place. I look at innovation as an approach." Dean of London Business School, Sir Andrew Likerman

"Innovation, the process of having original ideas and insights that have value; then implementing them. It is easier to name what stifles innovation and how to kill creativity – like rigid structure and high stress." President of Olin College of Engineering, Richard Miller

"Innovation doesn't have to be about creating the next iPad. It can be the way you treat a customer." Mr. Joe Caruso

"Innovation is creative problem solving." Proctor and Gamble's Director of External Relations, Ellen Bawan

Innovation and learning come in many forms. There are interchangeable insights that run through the common roots of both. When innovation and learning are meaningful, Wagner often found non-traditional approaches are used for traditional problems.

Kirk Phelps, a successful innovator and master learner noted his learning environment was mostly non-traditional, supported by parents who were comfortable with a trial and error approach that did not include criticism and judgment. As a child his parents did not care if he was on a winning team or not. They just wanted him to experience different kinds of people and develop an interest in sports. Wagner states, "You cannot innovate from nothing, you must have some knowledge; though how much knowledge you need, when you need it, and how best to acquire it are important questions."

Kirk Phelps told Wagner, "What you study is not that important. Knowing how to find things is way more important (integration on a personal level)." What tools did I want to add to my toolbox? My parents didn't care all that much about what I was interested in, they were far more interested in the process of experiencing learning. Explore, experiment and discuss through trial and error – to take risks and to fall down without criticism supports learning.

M.I.T.'s Joost Bonson told Wagner, "Being innovative is central (natural) to being human – we are all playful and curious animals, until it is pounded out of us." How true, how true this is when approaches to learning are not brain-compatible!

After he researched the topic of meaningful learning Wagner said, "I now understand that the qualities of innovation include:

- Perseverance
- Willingness to experiment
- Take risks
- Tolerated failure
- Design thinking
- Critical thinking
- These are all elements that outweigh subject content."

In another of Tony Wagner's books, *The Global Achievement Gap*, he suggests seven (7) survival skills for continuous, lifelong learning.

1. Problem solving
2. Calibration
3. Adaptability
4. Finding and analyzing information
5. Intuition
6. Effective oral and written communications
7. Curiosity and imagination

These elements on Wagner's two (2) lists are all found in brain-compatible learning environments, as are the skills Jeff H. Dyer, Hal B. Gregerson, and Clayton M. Christensen wrote about in their article *The Innovator's DNA* (Harvard Business Review). They divided these skills into two (2) categories – Doing and Thinking.

DOING:

Questions: Allows individuals to consider new possibilities

Observing: Detects new ways of doing things

Experimenting: Tries new experiences an explores the world

Networking: Gains radically different views from diverse backgrounds

THINKING:

Association: Puts together the four (4) patterns of "doing" which cultivates innovation and learning.

Judy Gilbert, Director of Talent at Google stated, "Of course we look for smarts, but intellectual curiosity is more important. We look for someone who questions how they can make something better. David Kelly, founder of IDEO, a global design firm, has the slogan "fail early and fail often."

Wagner points out the importance of play with his statement, "observe, explore, imagine and learn through play more than we would ever have thought possible." Alison Gopnik (University of California, Berkley) discuss progression of play from passion to purpose, through opportunities to explore by trial and error – play is brain-compatible learning.

It is a poor concept to feel that all a model had to do was act in a certain way and attempts to imitate them would help learners to do likewise. The joy of learning is based on experiencing all the stages (the ups and downs) of preparation. Struggle is nature's indirect approach and preparation for learning. Efficient preparation develops flexible knowledge and portable skills (innovation). Preparation and struggle are two (2) of the most important stages of long-term progress; they are often overlooked and undervalued.

You cannot engineer innovation, but you can increase the odds of it occurring. Innovation broadly defined is the critical ingredient when learning. Learning development approaches produce what is considered the raw material of innovation and learning environments that encourage diversity (not sameness), experimentation (not following), risk taking (not trying to get-it-right), and combining skills from many fields (not staying home) do what? The rest of the thought is missing.

The culture of teaching to get-it-right does not support this kind of innovation. It lacks wide ranging curiosity and support for the kind of continuous learning that is vital to growth. Formal answers do matter, but real life experiences are often more valuable. The opportunity to draw from a wide range of diverse experiences can generate many breaks through ideas and insights.

The concept of "disruptive innovation" in the 1987 book, *The Innovations Diploma,* points to the value of 1. Questioning, 2. Experimenting, 3. Associating and 4. Networking.

1. Curiosity (Questioning)
2. Risk taking (Experimenting)
3. Linking concepts from different intellectual mash-ups, disciplines (Association)
4. A search for new ideas (Networking)

"Innovators engage in these mental activities regularly, it is a habit." Hal B. Gregerson – author of *The Innovators DNA*. Steven Jobs, perhaps one of the most innovative men the world has ever seen said, "Be curious, experiment, take risks, stay hungry, and stay foolish."

Walter Isaacson, author of the book *Steve Jobs*, said there was a difference between intelligence and genius and Jobs was more genius. He had imaginative leaps that were instinctive, unexpected and at times magical. They were sparked by intuition, not analytical rigor.

Isaacson said Jobs came to value experiential wisdom over empirical analysis. He didn't study data or crunch numbers but could sense what lay ahead. Jobs appreciated the power of intuition, in contrast to what he called "western rational thought" (Isaacson's words).

Steve Jobs' intuition was based not on conventional learning, but on experiential wisdom. He had a lot of imagination and knew how to apply it. As Einstein said, "imagination is more important than knowledge. " Bill Gates was super smart, Jobs was super ingenious and enjoyed the concept of applying creativity that spawned innovations that changed the world.

Thinking

The only species on earth that thinks about their thoughts is the human race. What is being discussed here I hope will spark an interest in thinking about our thoughts when it comes to acts of learning.

The nature of learning is very efficient, allowing us to think constructively. To picture; to imagine; to wonder what-if; are all valuable thinking components of the kind of learning that go beyond just knowing facts.

In brain-compatible learning environments playfulness and imagination support a journey of learning that students would otherwise not have available to them. Meaningful learning is an adventure on the way to things true or untrue, that students may not have been expected.

The nature of learning and information delivery systems is supported by a culture that is benevolent, tolerant, understanding, flexible and positive about unwanted outcomes. On the other hand some approaches to learning are based on a culture that views poor outcomes as failure and not as the invaluable feedback that nature intended them to be.

Modernized approaches to learning have nothing fancy, complicated, or frustrating about them. Within this culture students are given the opportunity to rethink their relationship with the trial and error risks that are clearly important components of change and development. Modernized approaches to learning are in harmony with how the brain has previously wired itself for learning. The vitamin RSTD supports progress:

- **R**ecalling

- **S**urviving

- **T**hriving

- **D**eveloping

If we believe that preventing useful information from reaching students is a bad thing, it then follows that keeping information about the brain's connection to learning from students and teachers would also be damaging. When something starts – it normally has an end. One exception is the process of learning, which never ends. Learning is a life-long tour of experiences and more than a quick visit to facts.

When things have come together, the brain had done it first. Some approaches to learning overlook that process. Valuable insights about the brain's connection to the nature of learning are common knowledge to researchers from several fields of science. These studies often provoke controversy and rejection when they surface beyond the scholarship of respected studies.

Research has shown that putting aside some out-of-date, traditional approaches to learning can provide paths to improving approaches to learning. But this new research can also cause debates by individuals who prefer to hold onto what is no longer seen as being as useful and meaningful as it once was.

Approaches to learning that are being used by both providers and receivers of information should be designed and structured to keep individuals efficiently and playfully involved in the game of learning. When it comes to the game of learning, the game could stand for "Giving Anyone More Enjoyment." This can be accomplished by pulling back the curtain and revealing what is being overlooked when it comes to taking advantage and leveraging the brain's connection to learning.

The human brain is the gateway to learning and, for better or worse, approaches to learning are the gate-keepers. The human brain is capable of accepting signals of information from the environment, which includes the body in which it lives. Some useful signals will arrive without conscious effort. There is also information that we seek coming into the brain. Decisions and prediction about this incoming information are being made based on our prior knowledge and past experiences.

Notes from Harvard
"The mind, body, and the self" – Mary Helen Immordino Yang

The following section contains some of the notes I made while attending Harvard University's Connecting Mind-Brain to Education Institute in 2010, 2011 and 2012. My suggestion is to use my notes to create your own insights and story about each point.

Harvard's Connecting Mind-Brain to Education Institute has joined information about the biology of human development with information from cognitive science to gain positive results when learning. The modern model of the human mind puts the brain as the organ that carries most of the learning. The fundamental nature of a person is contained in their brain. The body also contributes to learning, as does a person's environment in shaping learning and providing information.

Research centers and scientists are tying biology, cognitive sciences, and human development together with education to create scientific groundwork for teaching and learning. We now have a large and growing database about learning thanks to the work of many practitioners and researchers who create a story of scientific content that enhances acts of learning.

Kurt Fischer[24]
Topic; building a better model for learning to replace the many myths that exist

- Train the brain to do what it wants to do - learn efficiently. To provide optimal support for learning requires knowledge of how emotions influence learning.

---

[24] Director of Harvard University's Connecting the Mind-Brain to Education Institution

- Developing and learning are not a linear process. Learning is a web of connections in the brain. (The brain operates like a committee, with most members having their say all at the same time).
- In less than a second after we see a word; language, emotions, etc., just about everything comes into play.
- The brain is a parallel processor. Simultaneously the brain evaluates incoming information with past experiences to determine what is safe – unsafe, useful – un-useful etc. This occurs before information will be encoded in long-term memory.
- Things that effect to our learning include: anger, fear, emotional evaluation, and our perceptions.
- The brain wants to act efficiently, using the smallest amount of energy it can. Unskilled individuals use more brain activity, which, is less efficient.
- We self-build and construct knowledge when learning. Learning is a dynamic, active process that takes time. Learning is developmental.
- 1896-1936 John Dewey believed schools and teachers should study learning.
- Learning happens in networks throughout the brain, during emotional evaluation.
- We learn through a history of questions. We grasp and build with our minds' past experiences.
- The whole brain resonates robust learning through different brain processes.
- Research informs practice and practice informs research.
- Often good courses can produce poor learning, with little evidence of understanding, problem solving or learning.
- Use implicit models (personal models, non-external) and metaphors.
- It is our experiences that hold understanding together.

- When learning, it is useful to know that functions can improve to optimal, but will often fall off. (The gap is larger for adults). We regress and then rebuild.
- We learn in domains and in context.
- Unfortunately fast learning produces rigid forms.
- Over time, slow learning produces more variables and flexibility.
- Our actions build representations and abstractions within the networks of the brain. The body contributes to learning, providing information that shapes learning.

Myths Include:
Males and females have fundamentally different brains.
Knowledge is something that we give to each other.
Learning is about filling the brain with information.
There are left and right brain learners.
We only use 10% of our brain.
Link to Kurt Fischer

http://www.uknow.gse.harvard.edu/learning/learning002b.html

Mary Helen Immordino Yang, Ed.D[25]

Topic: The body, mind & the self. Learning process is social, psychological, & emotional. We feel, therefore we learn. Birds fly, fish swim, humans feel.

- Learning is influenced by culture and customs. All background information (past experiences) influences new learning.

---

[25] Professor of Education of Psychology Brain and Creativity Institute University of Southern California

- Having compassion for pain, admiration for skills, and admiration for virtue (social, physical, psychological) supports learning.
- Emotions change the whole body-brain system by releasing chemicals.
- Change the way people come to learning, it starts in the brain.
- Any idea between two people is an emotional experience. It is social interactions that can lead to new learning.
- Learning is not about information. It is about developing the ability to see options, using and constructing knowledge personal in nature.
- **Coverage** - Giving out information is referred to as coverage and this does not develop meaningful new learning.
- **Motivation** - Intrinsic motivation or self-motivation and learning for the fun of it is more useful than extrinsic motivation, or learning for what you can get or learning to please others.
- Have receivers of information explain what they are learning and how it can be used in several different ways, this will help to encode long-term meaningful learning.
- Change the way individuals come to learning, make learning environments emotionally safe.

Link to Mary Helen Immordino-Yang on TED Talks
www.youtube.com/watch?v=RViuTHBIOq8

Dr. David Rose[26]

Topic: Students are only learning disabled in some environments. The learning environment is the problem, not the student. Progress and a lack of learning are both the results of interactions and of biology (chemicals) in the brain.

- Brains are individual; all learners have individual brains.
- All learners may be learning the same topic, but in different parts of the brain.
- The brain is always learning and rewiring its web of connection. Learning is making a new connection within the brain. Learning is mostly non-conscious.
- In the brain: recognition, strategies, engagement are taking place.
- **Recognition** – We perceive information, and then the brain rejects some, and then turns what is left into usable knowledge, based on past experiences.
- **Strategies** – Use information in play or game like actions.
- **Engagement** – Finding a means for future use of information.
- Design approaches to learning so that they are a means of personal expression and a means of enjoyment for the student.
- Providing options and giving choices in the learning environment is a brain-compatible approach to learning and improving.
- Unwanted outcomes are a biochemical requirement of meaningful learning. They are valuable feedback for future reference.
- Unwanted outcomes are a means of expression that cultivates abilities.

---

[26] Chief Scientist, Chief Education Officer, Cognition and Learning Center for Applied Learning, Harvard Graduate School of Education.

- Unwanted outcomes should be introduced into learning environments.

Link to Dr. Rose: http://www.cast.org/about/staff/drose.html

David Perkins, Ph.D[27]
Topic: Knowledge to Go

Ideally knowledge is not something we give to each other. It should be seen as knowledge to go:

Knowledge to think about

Knowledge to think with

Knowledge to see and act with

- Go from knowledge about information to acting with information.
- Learning is making something more out of something basic.
- Personal knowledge is what will be retrieved.
- Find what makes information matter to students, but prior perceptions can interfere.
- Meaningful Learning: Learned in one area, but can be used in different areas.[28]
- Passive Conceptual Vocabulary: (non-active, not personalized) is useless, but can be helped by questions.

There is Fast and Slow Cognition

Slow: Planning – a controlled processing.

---

[27]Professor of Teaching and Learning Harvard Graduate School of Education.

[28] Thorndike 1923, Woodworth 1903

Fast: A doing-mind – automatic processing.

Slow: Deliberate

Fast: Rapid pattern recognition, quick, intuitive assembly.

Fast: Cognition keeps summarizing and finding options.

Slow: Can give a report. (If you try to assemble action it can get lost!)

Fast: You see results – just-do-it (a non-conscious process).

Fast: Pattern crystallization.

Fast: What to do? Maybe this, imagine it. Fast cognition just keeps swimming.

- Often unworkable answers and outcomes have been over thought and under learned!
- If you look at an iceberg; some ice is above the water but most of this mountain of ice is below the water line. The ice below the water keeps what can be seen above the water in balance. See the ice below the water as our non-conscious mind that holds a larger volume of information made up of our past experiences encoded for future use non-consciously influencing new learning. New learning is supported by prior knowledge.
- We must move on from threshold ideas and look outward into the world, but not for details.

      Be creative

Start with an idea

See it as a tool

Then use it.

- The brain is a self-organizing system.
- Within the brain, learning changes how genes express themselves, influenced by experiences and the environment.

- Every time our eyes move new information arrives, changing what we perceive. Our perceptions have implications for learning.
- Perceptions are about survival; they are a generalization, a variable that begins with the eye and is then constructed.
- The brain pays attention to change. The brain non-consciously sees edges and contrasts automatically.
- Black and white pictures are encoded faster than color pictures which provide less personal information.
- What we currently know shapes our perceptions.

Link to David Rose: http://www.gse.harvard.edu/directory/faculty/faculty-detail/?fc=260&flt=b&sub=all

Kurt Fischer

Topic: Dynamics of Learning

- When something is said to be really known, it is not known in just one way.
- At times there is learned content – but without problem solving, seeing options, critical thinking opportunities – absolutes stay undeveloped.
- Use metaphors and implicit personal models to develop abilities.
- Knowledge varies with how much contextual support was available.
- The brain takes in more than it needs, then will prune what is not selected for survival, or does not work efficiently to accomplish low energy use.
- Central vision sends different information to the brain than peripheral vision – which is better for automatically processing motion to save energy. Centered vision is slow and is good for details.

- Many broad facts about learning from thirty years ago have been found to be no longer true. Key discoveries have changed the understanding of how development and learning involve direct contributions from our DNA and genetic mechanisms.

L. Todd Rose [29]

Topic: The importance of working memory.

- Working memory has the ability to hold and manipulate information for a short period of time in your brain. It is the foundation for planning, organization and goal directed behavior. (Example: Hearing numbers, and then holding them in mind while we do a task.)
- While a large body of empirical research clearly demonstrates there is a connection between working memory and learning, this knowledge is rarely communicated to those that need it the most – educators and policy makers.
- The brain is goal directed (survival). Goals drive attention, perceptions and learning. There are outcome goals and process goals – which are more valuable for learning.
- Personal representations lead to concepts for learning, but they must be in context.
- Random or variability-driven learning leads to accomplishing innovation.

---

[29] Research scientist – Center for Applied Learning, Harvard Lecturer on Learning.

Jane Holmes Bernstein Ph.D[30]

Topic: Learning

- Unfortunately, since the 12th century, little has changed in teaching.
- Development is not linear.
- Teach the same concept in a different way.
- Individuals have their own goals.
- Education should be for early advancement of thinking skills.
- The topic of learning is about behavior.
- Self-management is important.
- The first four years of a child's life are for play, not for learning to read.
- Seeing individuals as learners has shifted to seeing individuals as the owner of the learning organ (brain) – a biological organism influenced by behavior in environments.
- See the whole person – go beyond cognition.
- Brains get built, they are wired during interactions. The brain is necessary, but it is not self-sufficient, it needs interaction.
- Individuals must be biologically (or developmentally) ready to gain understanding of use of information.
- Introduce problems through play.
- Brains do not operate in isolation – they need context.

Context:

A Physical Context: external world, internal tools

A Psychological Context: historical context, cultural setting, social context, emotional experiences (feelings, beliefs, goals, values)

A Narrative Context: Logical/quantitative, existential, hands on, interpersonal/collaboration, aesthetic, words
http://f1000.com/prime/thefaculty/member/8260755542511366

---

30 Harvard Medical School

Howard Gardner[31]

Topic: Intelligence

- Intelligence is putting things to use in many ways. Learning is learning a lot of ways.
- Multiple Intelligences is a means, not an end.
- Gardner's Multiple Intelligences: **Logical-Mathematical Intelligence / Linguistic Intelligence / Spatial Intelligence / Musical Intelligence / Bodily-Kinesthetic Intelligence / The Personal Intelligences / Intrapersonal intelligence.**
- Teach the individual, personalize education.
- **Intelligence:** The potential to process information in certain ways in order to solve problems or fashion outcomes.
- We learn by doing things.
- Anything worth learning should be shared in multiple ways and you will reach more and make more sense.
- Create learning environments that require using different intelligences.
- Create search light minds vs. listening minds.
- The brain is smarter than we are.
- Be metacognitive; learning about learning.
- Use ongoing assessments not standardized tests.
- Teach for understanding.

Link to Howard Gardner:

http://en.wikipedia.org/wiki/Howard_Gardner

---

[31] Harvard Graduate School of Education

Re-Thinking Possibilities

"Many people who had difficulty learning in the past might have prospered if these new ideas about efficient instruction had been available."[32]

Despite the efforts of well-meaning educators, parents, coaches, employers and instructors, many individuals who are trying to learn are struggling.

Educational researchers, Caine and Caine point out,

"Meaningful learning involves acknowledging the brain's rules for learning and keeping those rules in mind." Jay Matthews, "21st century learning is not new; it represents what our best educators have been doing for several centuries."[33], "the elements of effective lessons have been with us for thousands of years." [34] Dylan William Perhaps some of today's approaches to sharing information need a re-start button!

Tad James M.S, Ph.D said, "We use internal processing strategies for everything we do. All of our apparent external behaviors are controlled by internal processing strategies. It's what somebody does in their brain and nervous system that produces a result," states Roberta Gates, Educator.

Approaches to learning that are described as being in the education business may not be as successful as approaches to learning that see themselves as being in the student business. Elle Brothers, the president of the very successful American Girl Company, said while her company sells millions of dolls, she is not in the doll business; she is in the little girl business. When approaches to learning are in the business of helping students gain an education, they are more efficient than approaches that see themselves as being in the business of providing information.

---

[32] *How People Learn,* by Bransford, Brown, Cocking, 2000
[33] *Fuse,* by Jay Mathews, p. 25
[34] *Embedded Formative Assessment,* by Dylan Williams, p. 189

118

On the first day of a new school year, or the start of a business training program, or the beginning of sports instruction, perhaps teachers should start by telling their students that all students came into the world as capable self-learners and capable self-teachers and that as an educator they here to help students, invent their own reading, writing, math, golf or business skills. Then the pace of progress will be different from when students are just hoping to learn from the corrections and directions that teach-to-fix to get-it-right approaches to education offer.

In John Medina's book *Brain Rules* he noted the following insights from his research:

- Emotions make the brain pay attention. (p. 256)
- Our ability to learn is based on a series of increasingly self-connected ideas. (p. 270)
- We are always using pre-loaded information. (p. 267)
- New information "re-sculpts" prior information and sends the re-created whole back for new storage. The new information and the past information now act as if they were encountered together." (p. 129)

> *He who looks outside; dreams;*
> *He who looks inside, awakes.*
> Carl Gustav Jung

Learn-and-Develop Versus Teach-to-Fix

"Our desire is to incorporate the new discoveries about how the human brain learns, teaching in harmony with the human brain." Prof. Terry Doyle[35]

Rethinking my approach to teaching helped me to change from using a teacher-centered teach-to-fix to get something right

---
[35] *Helping Students Learn in a Learner Centered Environment,* p 36

approach, to a brain-compatible, student-centered learn-and-develop approach.

This was a new approach for me; one that is proactive, and after basic core information is understood, does not focus on trying to fix unwanted outcomes. It is an approach that is supporting self-discovery, self-regulation, and self-reliance skills. Spending time on a task is only one element of learn-and-develop approaches.

The kind of stress that slows learning normally exists in a teach-to-fix to get-it-right environment. I use the terms "teach-to-fix to get-it-right" vs. "learn-and-develop." Terry Doyle, (Chief Instructor at Ferris State University Faculty Center for Teaching and Learning), uses the terms "teacher-centered environment" vs. "learner-centered environments" in his book *Helping Students Learn in a Learner Centered Environment.* Terry states, "Our desire is to incorporate the new discoveries about how the human brain learns, teaching in harmony with the human brain."

Learn-and-develop environments have jumping off points that are not available in teach-to-fix approaches. Efficient acts of learning often do not rely on rational or logical approaches to insights and answers on which teach-to-fix environments are often founded. Student-centered learn-and-develop approaches to progress allow our current observations and beliefs to interact with our previous experiences. The nature of learning uses cross-disciplinary reasoning and deduction skills, grounded in past personal experiences.

Studies show there is a need for what could be called a "wonder" approach to learning that uses what-if thinking that is self-evident to the nature of learning. Learn-and-develop approaches to improving use an "autobiographical" personal path to make sense of the world in ways that others do not. Self-organization and adaptive mimicking support learning and developing while applying core information.

Brain-compatible information delivery systems help students to make personal sense of the environment. I would describe the brain's operating principles by saying: **human beings of all ages learn by doing, observing the outcome, then adjusting if needed, based on past experiences.** Prof. Peter Atkins said something similar, "Humanity makes observation then compares notes."[36]

The knack of rethinking; the knack of seeing more options; the knack of developing other usages for information; are all born in learn-and-develop environments free of judgments while promoting self-organization, self-development and self-evaluation.

At the core of the nature of learning is mankind's natural drive, or intent to do and to learn (to survive). Research points out that *to-do* intent always precedes ability. One purpose of nature's biological intent (or plan) for learning is to indirectly prepare functions that will become fully operative much later. There are teach-to-fix environments that suppress mankind's natural intent to do by sidestepping the use of the indirect preparation (past experiences) by giving how-to directions.

Teach-to-fix environments often mute curiosity and dilute imagination with passive, non-invasive, approaches to learning. On the other hand, efficient student-centered learn-and-develop environments are safe and active, as individuals learn more from ever-changing environments by using real time interactions with basic information.

Student-centered learn-and-develop approaches pull the indirect preparation of past experiences forward; mixing them with what is taking place now. Efficient use of past experiences brings out autobiographical images and personal visions that support the kind of learning that lasts.

Some students are the authors of their own demise when they make poor assumptions about teach-to-fix environments and the directions and corrections they provide. When all is said and done, there is often more being *said* than *being accomplished* by students in teach-to-fix environments.

---

[36] *Physical Chemistry* by Peter Atkins and Julio de Paula, p. 11 (Lincoln College, Oxford University)

Some students are always trying to fix something and this can be why learning that lasts is not taking hold. **Fixing is attractive to the emotional needs of a student's mind.** Hopefully, the emotional mind will learn that there is no failure, only usable feedback for future reference. Progress and change from learn-and-develop approaches to education tend to stay around and not just a novelty of occasional success. Unfortunately, teach-to-fix environments can foster a damaging *fixing* mentality promoting students to attempt perfection that can last a lifetime.

Learn-and-develop environments support using one's personal genius, uncovering the creative potential of individuals that teach-to-fix environments do not promote. Individuals often find themselves caught in the haze of how-to directions from a perceived expert and not at the hub of self-organized creative insights, which can guide a learn-and-develop journey in the direction of progress.

Some things learned by rote are normally half-understood and imperfectly felt. (This is force-fed information.)

I realize that it will take time to change the powerful assumptions about teach-to-fix environments that have perceived experts delivering how-to statements to individuals who want to make progress. "If mental models drive the decisions that we all make, the implication is that in order to successfully improve education we have to change the mental model that educators have of learning and teaching."[37]

A learn-and-develop approach to education is shaping a student's interest and enthusiasm for seeing options that enhance their ability to ask useful questions. These approaches to learning also recognize that silent personal insights are very valuable for sustained progress. In learn-and-develop environments growth is

---

[37] Caine and Caine, p.22

just ahead, with solutions from the adaptive skills of curiosity, imagination and what-if ideas unleashing the student's creative potential. "Plato reasoned that the most important knowledge was already inside the student. Therefore, the role of the teacher was to facilitate the student's realization of this inner one's knowing through a quest that leads to independent thought."[38] I refer to this realization of inner knowledge as *out*-struction – drawing on past experiences – as opposed to *in*struction.

Efficient approaches to learning help individuals invent and create their own reasoning and destructive and problem solving skills. Meaningful acts of learning rarely rely upon the completely rational or linear approach to answers on which teach-to-fix environments are normally founded.

Learn-and-develop approaches to progress allow our current observations to creatively interact with our previous experiences. Studies show that the nature of learning uses cross-disciplinary reasoning and deduction skills, (based on past personal experiences), that can be overlooked in teach-to-fix environments.

Teach-to-fix approaches to progress normally do not give students the opportunity to make up their own minds. The opportunity to choose may be the most important element to gaining a good education.

How-to directions in teach-to-fix environments can reach such abstraction that valuable core subject knowledge gets lost, thereby suppressing a huge number of useful personal questions and insights. On the other hand, learn-and-develop environments have the ability to illuminate the kind of reference points and associations that make what may seem difficult, easy. Learn-and-develop environments expand established patterns and create new personal pathways for putting new information together.

Learn-and-develop approaches to education provide a quality learning experience by focusing on three-dimensional integrated learning (mental intelligence, physical intelligence, and

---

[38] *Think Creatively*, by Michael Gelb, p. 33

emotional intelligence) for enhanced learning ability. By staying aware of these three areas of intelligence and the brain's five major learning systems, (Reflection, Action, Intention, Social, Passion) one can gain valuable insights into the nature of learning and long-term progress.

In learn-and-develop environments students are active participants in their own learning, they are sharing their information and they are practicing their learning with the educator.

At this stage of education students connect the learning to their world. If learning is not personally meaningful, the information will not be remembered. **The age-old question, "How are you going to use this?" must be answered and this is often the forgotten part of approaches to learning.**

In their book, *Education on the Edge of Possibility,* Renate and Geoffrey Caine point out some new ways of evaluating approaches to learning and teaching. Their insights are founded on research about the brain, questioning many of the public's and some educators' deepest assumptions about education. These assumptions, for the most part, are based on teach-to-fix approaches to learning that see educators and perceived experts as owning information that they then pass on. These teach-to-fix environments are not as efficient as we once thought them to be for encoding for long-term learning (retention). In teach-to-fix environments individuals are asked to focus on getting-it-right or how to do something and subsequently avoid self-discover experiences.

On the other hand, an inside to outside approach to learning develops insights about core concepts. These approaches move away from details and move on to basic core information allowing any details that follow to be in accordance with one's own individual make-up. Contemplate this: Core concepts are based on the environment. We shoot basketballs up because the basket is up. Any details of shooting up follow that basic core concept. When details lead, as they do in teach-to-fix learning environments it can take a long time to learn or may never take hold.

In learn-and-develop environments individuals are always given the freedom to self-organize and learn through being open to all possibilities. This is an opportunity to make up their mind. The Caines' point out that these approaches to learning develop individuals who are self-confident and can be in charge when left on their own. It seems these self-organizers are happy with themselves and their skills. Their creative and innovative thinking skills put them in great demand in the workplace.

Learning does not develop from scratch. Comparisons, associations, and parallels promote learning. When first learning a basic skill, the foundation for learning that skill is formed when the brain sees parallel relationships in past experience. Long-term learning is not normally formed through memorization, doing drills, or copying expert models. Hopefully, as individuals encounter new insights, it will lead them to the kind of curiosity and use of imagination that develop know-how skills that are personal in nature. Change, transition, or modification occurs at a rich, deep, lasting level when attempts to make progress are cross referenced with past experiences that have been self-organized in learn-and-develop environments. As cognitive scientists say, the more parallels and association, the merrier.

Efficient learn-and-develop environments are less concerned with outcome results than the development of the performing "self." **Learning starts to take hold when we master nature's most basic opportunity for learning, which is *just do something*.** As sure as night is normally dark and day is normally light, learning beckons the law of chance. Without chance and doing there are no new beginnings.

Today, anything I write, say, or demonstrate is not trying to teach. I am doing the best I can to enhance learning potential by passing on some food for thought that may influence readers, listeners, and on-lookers to exchange some of their current insights for new ones about self-discovery, learning and the brain connection to this process.

For thousands of years, when mankind woke up in the morning, our ancestors' brains were wired to look for food for their bodies and an activity that was food for their minds. If food for the body had always been given to man, mankind would not have self-developed this ability to find food and he would not have survived. Likewise, if our ancestors did not have the opportunity to self-develop the steps and stages of solving problems (food for the mind), they would have not survived. But humankind has survived through the development of the self.

Learn-and-develop environments recapture one's childhood, where acts of curiosity lead to learning that lasts. **When educators use words, symbols, or phrases for their own purpose, they often miss the needs of the students.** The structure and design of learning environments that are expected to be efficient must be influenced by the needs of the individuals they are serving.

The core of meaningful learning is more about improvising and inventing than following directions. The intention of teach-to-fix environments is normally to promote their ideas, as they overlook the value of self-discovery by students as accommodations to the task at hand. John Taylor Gatto, award-winning educator, stated in his book *Dumbing Us Down*, "The truth is that some schools don't really teach anything except how to obey orders. We've built a way of life that depends on people doing what they are told, because they don't know how to tell themselves what to do. That's the biggest lesson I teach."

Learning Styles

Many long held views about learning are being un-thought in the 21st century. University of Virginia cognitive psychologist Daniel Willingham published research in 2005 that showed we should teach to the content of the subject, not to a learning style. Then seven years later a Wall Street Journal article by Professors

Christopher Chabrs (Union College) and Daniel Semour (Univ. of Illinois) revisited the Learning Style Theory along with two other brain myths.

They began their article with three statements asking which one was false:

1) We only use 10% of our brain.
2) Overly stimulated environments will increase the intelligence of preschool children.
3) Individuals learn better when they receive information in their preferred learning style.

It turns out all three statements are false!

- The article pointed out that two hundred and forty-two teachers took part in a study by Sanne Dekker and colleagues at the Universities of Amsterdam and of Bristol. The findings report that the most popular brain myth was about learning styles. Ninety four percent (94%) of the teachers in the study believed they should teach to the student's learning style.
- Forty seven percent (47%) believed that we only use ten percent (10%) of our brain, while contemporary studies show that we use the entire brain.
- Seventy six percent (76%) believe that exposure to Baby Einstein type video enrichment and going beyond what is already a significant developmental environment would improve a child's cognitive development – which is not true.

The Association for Psychological Science found that there is essentially no evidence that customizing instruction to match a student's preferred learning style will lead to better achievement.

Daniel Willingham's research shows that teachers should teach to the content's modality, not the student's learning style. If you want students to see something; or hear something; or feel something, teach for that outcome, not to a preferred learning style. Kampwirth and Bates, 1980; Arter and Jenkins 1979; Kavale and Forness 1987, all found similar results.

"Why do people believe in a theory that has no research behind it? They believe because it fits a general assumption; or because others believe the theory; or because it is perceived to have become common knowledge? In 1979 researchers Arter and Jenkins reported that more than ninety percent (90%) of special education teachers believed in the Learning Styles theory."
Daniel Willingham

An Assumption

I assume that the aim of teachers, coaches, parents, employers and all other information providers is to share ideas that are educational; ideas that individuals can use and from which they can learn. This hypothesis brings on a question: How is education defined and what kinds of ideas have proven to be the most educational or the best for learning? Let's define learning the way some cognitive scientists do: "Learning is a beneficial biochemical change."

Hold on, are we making this conversation more detailed than it needs to be? Not really. When we say, "I know this or that" or "I can demonstrate what I know" or "I can recall information or a skill," learning is not being demonstrated, only a performance of what has been learned is observable. We see the result of a process, but not the process.

Learning is an internal biochemical process that is influenced by a number of things including information, environments in which information exists, the manner in which the information is being shared, emotions and the past experiences of the receivers of information. The ideas that appear to be the most educational include:

- Ideas that make sense and have meaning to a receiver of information.
- Ideas that support meaningful learning tend to be proactive; free of negative criticism.
- Ideas that are valuable and educational can cause an exchange of poor insights for useful ones.

Approaches to learning cause the release of chemicals throughout our nervous system, including the brain. Some approaches to learning release chemicals that can support learning and some approaches release the kind of chemicals that suppress learning. This reality is repeated throughout this book.

Learning should not be seen as an event. Learning is a process that develops over time. Our biological possibilities are revealed during a journey of discovery, or during the process of learning and not in the observable outcomes of our interactions with our environment.

Unfortunately, approaches to learning are often focused on fixing the outcome. Studies into the nature of learning on the other hand would suggest that we adjust the approach to learning that is being used. Learning is not just about information. Learning to think well, learning to reason, learning to enhance deduction skills and learning to see options all take precedence over information when it comes to life-long learning.

This may be a counterintuitive view; "perhaps in time the so called Dark Ages will be thought of as including our own." George C. Lichtenberg

In SMART, SAFE, PLAYFUL environments, learning to make progress is more about anticipating outcomes than judgments of results.

<u>S.M.A.R.T. CLASSROOMS</u> =
<u>S</u>tudents' <u>M</u>inds <u>A</u>re Really Talented

In smart classrooms, no student is seen as broken and in need of fixing, unwanted outcomes are not judged, criticized or seen as failure, but are viewed as valuable feedback for future reference. In these environments teachers realize that every student is on a journey of development and their present skills and information base are exactly where they should be, nothing is missing, it is just developing. These individuals should be producing unwanted outcomes when learning.

The numbers we know before entering school (0 to 10) are the same numbers that build rocket ships; over time we just learned to do something different with them. We could say the same about the letters of the alphabet.

<u>S.A.F.E.</u> =
<u>S</u>tudents <u>A</u>lways <u>F</u>irst <u>E</u>nvironment ™

There are learning environments where students are told what's wrong and they don't feel safe. This approach is a negative reaction to unwanted outcomes and is not a proactive safe learning experience that promotes an individual's self-confidence. A brain-compatible information delivery system recognizes that the main job of any provider of information is to make receivers of information feel smart and self-confident, not to focus on unworkable outcomes.

<u>P.L.A.Y.F.U.L.</u> CLASSROOMS =
<u>P</u>owerful <u>L</u>earning <u>A</u>bout <u>Y</u>ourself <u>F</u>inds <u>U</u>seful <u>L</u>earning ™

Progress and improvement are grounded in the "self" found in self-reliance, one of the many self-skills human beings have when learning is based on play. We clearly play to learn, we did not have to learn to play.

The following are some traits that can cause a negative bio-chemical emotional state:

- Trying to please others when learning
- Hearing negative criticism from ourselves or others when learning
- Seeing unwanted outcomes as failure when learning
- Comparing one's self to others when learning
- Trying to get-it-right when learning

When individuals are not learning and making progress at a reasonable pace, what would make things more learnable for use beyond classrooms, sports practice fields and business seminars? That of course is the sixty-four thousand dollar question for any giver or taker of information who wants to move in the direction of peak personal learning experiences.

"Learning is more efficient when using a learning plan than a course outline. Learning is also more efficient when guided by a process structure, than by a content structure."
Malcolm Knowle
Suggestion: Use brain-compatible information delivery systems found in 21st century learn-and-develop environments.

Scan tag or go to: You Tube: "Negative corrective have to fix things" – nlglive.com

Ten Things

Adapted from *Making Connection: Teaching and the Human Brain,* by Caine and Caine

"How individuals learn, often is never examined by a vast number of educators or the public."
Caine and Caine

1. **Every brain is unique.** Just as there are no two people exactly alike, no two brains are exactly alike. Just as our fingerprints and personalities are different, so are our brains.
2. **Enrichment and novelty are important to brain growth.** Each time you learn or do something new, your brain cells (neurons) make new connections. Our brains like things **that are novel (new). Novelty helps to keep things interesting!**
3. **Emotions are important to learning.** Emotions during a new learning experience influence our recall of this -
4. **The brain searches for patterns and meaning.** When we learn something new, we need to be able to hook that learning onto something we already know.
5. **The mind/body connection has an impact on learning.** Learning can be greatly influenced by how we feel physically.
6. **We have social brains.** Learning is a social event. We learn by watching, listening and talking to others.
7. **High stress or threats have a negative impact on learning.** Too much stress can actually damage your brain cells.
8. **We have different brain pathways for different memories.** Color, movement, rhythm, etc., simultaneously influence different arenas of the brain.

9. **The brain is complex and adaptive.** The brain adapts to different environments.
10. **Our brains go through various developmental stages.** There seem to be windows of opportunity or critical periods for learning different skills.

"Ignoring research based on the principles of learning can have negative effects on student learning."
Daniel T. Willingham, cognitive scientist, University of Virginia.

Bridges and Detours

Receivers of information in every age group have different backgrounds, varied past experiences and they are all at different developmental stages when it comes to learning. But there is an important common element that connects all these unique differences when it comes to the transference of information – a bridge that the approach to learning uses to connect providers to receivers of information.

What I am calling a bridge is the *manner* in which information is being shared with a receiver and also the *manner* in which a receiver approaches learning new information and skills. How efficient any transfer of information (bridge) can be is heavily influenced by the manner or culture, design and structure of approach to learning that is being used.

The approach that someone uses to transfer information is normally a direct reflection of what that individual knows and believes about the nature of learning. There are brain-compatible information delivery systems (bridges) that support meaningful improvement and there are approaches (bridges) that can create damaging detours *away* from learning. These damaging detours make learning and recalling information and skills difficult. Again, how information is being shared is either being done in a mind-brain-compatible manner or it is not.

Feedback

When long-term learning is the aim, brain-compatible approaches to learning evaluate what students should or should not be made aware of and what students should make themselves aware of. Some considerations that enhance learning include:

- Using metaphors
- Using real world environments with more than one solution
- Using more than one example to support findings
- Use a variety of points of view on a topic - both workable and unworkable
- Use comparisons and contrasts in different context

Phil Race, a professor of learning and teaching at Leeds Metropolitan University, discusses "feedback" in his book. He mentions attitudes that support efficient learning:

1. Want to learn
2. Need to learn
3. Learn by doing
4. Make sense
5. Learn from experience
6. Learn from assessment
7. Learn from feedback

Race suggests that individuals must:

- Recognize the need to learn
- Learn from trial and error

- Be able to make personal sense of information
- Learn from wanted and unwanted information
- Learn from self-exploration and self-assessment

The following statements are Race's suggestions related to Feedback:

<u>Feedback</u> should:

- Help individuals learn how to best use different kinds of environments as sources of information
- Help individuals see the big picture, not just details
- Provide overall information guidelines
- Help individuals see the real meaning of results
- Provide opportunities for clarification
- Help individuals recognize life differences and similarities
- Help individuals recognize strengths instead of weaknesses

Race based his suggestions on studies into the brain's connection to learning and how emotions influence that connection. At times, the feedback we receive is a non-conscious message.

New York Times columnist, David Brooks, wrote a book titled *The Social Animal*. It is a thesis on how human beings are influenced by the hidden workings of our non-conscious minds. Unknown to our conscious self, the power of deep, prior knowledge from our unconscious shapes the way we think and learn. Avoid the trap of thinking that decision making requires access to a lot of information and allow your non-conscious to kick-in and remove your conscious thinking self from the process. The mind often works best when it ignores some information.

"Intuitive, creative design-making relies on distilled experience.

More information can overwhelm the brain, making it harder to tap into core information."
Eric Kessler, Pace University

Design and Structure

"Often the problem is not a problem; it's the approach to the problem that is the problem." **Author Unknown**

Concerns and questions about a lack of progress, unwanted outcomes, or bad habits, tend to be personal in nature. For example, people ask, "Why am I not learning?" – "Why is my child not passing?" or "Why is it taking so long to learn this?" If these questions focused less on personal concerns and more on the design and structure of the approach that is being used to learn, there would be a greater number of positive learning experiences. **Studies show that one of the greatest influences on return on investment of the time and resources in the field of education is the design and structure of the approach to learning that is being used.**

Having developmentally appropriate designs and structures for making progress must be the aim of all learning environments. Are the subject content and the approach to sharing that content developmentally appropriate? That's a question worthy of investigation. Shared meanings between educators and students are important components of learning, and brain-compatible information delivery systems stay mindful of this.

The nature of learning is designed to move from not knowing to knowing by shifting from one set of unknowns and unpredictable experiences to the next, with each shift supporting a pattern of growth in intelligence. At the heart of brain-compatible learning is random shifting which is the biological plan that nature has for developing intelligence (instead of not trying to get something right).

Efficient approaches to education are normally **caretakers of learning skill,** (not teachers of subjects per say) as they improve the quality of questions people can ask of themselves and of others. Some questions can enhance learning, others do not.

Transfer

An efficient transfer of information from a source to a receiver encompasses many subtleties. Transfer is not inevitable. It is often overlooked that the cause of positive transfer is found in the design and structure of the information delivery system; the techniques related to planning and delivery of information. The aim is to successfully leverage new information.

"Near" or "low" transfer occurs when new learning situations closely resemble the original situation. This kind of learning transfer only holds up when the learning task is specific, or routine and consistent for procedural objectives.

"High" or "far" transfer occurs when one's existing knowledge can be applied to situations that vary from the initial learning situation. The key feature of "high" or "far" transfer is that it involves judgments about when and how knowledge is to be applied.

Information is said to be transferred when it can be applied in a variety of contexts, which requires seeing options and using reasoning and deduction skills.

Brain-compatible transfer provides new ways of solving old problems or challenges by mixing and layering past experiences that flow through new information to birth meaningful learning.

The nature of transfer with the brain in mind develops approaches that realize that it is important to avoid thinking in terms of an ideal model.

While these insights about transfer may seem counter-intuitive, it is a bare boned tightly linked transfer of information found in what-to-do basics that can lead to an orderly and meaningful conclusion for a participatory approach to learning anything.

When a journey of discovery is joined with what is already encoded in the brain from past experiences, it supports long-term learning. It is important that learning tasks differ from each other.

This allows students to extract more general information from each different task, thereby generating the transfer of learning strong support.

There is strong evidence that variability when practicing both simple tasks[39] and highly complex real life tasks[40] is important for learning. A sequence of different learning tasks always provides the backbone for a training program.

The Everyday Genius

Michael Alexander's preface to Peter Kline's book, *The Everyday Genius*, contains several insights that capture useful suggestions for enhancing acts of learning. Alexander starts by pointing out "in spite of the billions of dollars and millions of hours invested in education, for many students learning is often deferred." He went on to say, "This is a tragedy of enormous proportions, with terrible implications, but this does not have to continue. For the past three centuries, we were told that what teachers were doing was correct and we blamed students who failed to learn. But recently, rather than blaming students for not learning, researchers have been exploring the who, what, why, when and where of learning, pointing out that a teacher's every *move supports or detracts from the learning process. The total environment must be <u>orchestrated</u> to support learning.*"

What follows is based mostly on *The Everyday Genius*. It is a review of "integrative learning," based on research from Georgi Lozanov and others dating back to the 1950s.

- The main hypothesis of *The Everyday Genius* is that by changing the learning environment and the way information is presented, we can get substantially

---

[39] Paas and Van Merrienberg
[40] Shill, Vidal, Ployhart, Maragoni

better results than are possible with traditional approaches to education. **Traditional methods of teaching almost always fail to match the way we naturally learn.**

- Kline points out that **"the brain is an instrument (tool) that can be used either well or poorly.** It is not difficult to use it well, but many of the influences now in education condemn students to use their brains less efficiently than they could."

- The real cause of the problem is the culture of the system. Many students are hampered by outdated concepts of learning that often bring out the worst in both teachers and students. **This does not mean throwing out everything and starting over, it only suggests making better use of the new resources that are available now.**

- Maintaining the status quo will not benefit anyone, and fortunately changes are now available for improving approaches to learning. The reality is that it is important to **widen the circulation of information about optimum conditions for learning and how they can best be implemented.**

- The aim of "integrative learning" is to learn like children do. Although some new suggestions for enhancing acts of learning may seem childlike, they have been used with adults, and the learning was dramatic. **The same learning activities used by pre-schools were used by corporate executives.**

- The nature of learning and the brain's connection to this process of growth is so basic to the human experience that it has meaning at every level of the developmental process. **Most learning difficulties stem from ignoring this fundamental principle.**

Integrative learning is a seamless approach that recognizes that the development of the whole person must not be sacrificed for the development of a particular skill or intellectual progress. Some approaches to learning are discouraging which disempowers the student/learner.

- Learning without unpleasantness does not suggest learning without experiencing challenges and unwanted outcomes. Integrative learning recognizes the brain's connection to learning and therefore how important unwanted outcomes are for experiencing meaningful learning. **With a deeper understanding of the nature of learning, unwanted outcomes are no longer seen as failure; they become valuable feedback for future reference.**

- One of the keys to meaningful learning is to adapt the approach to learning that is used to the way we naturally learn. To educate, means "to lead out from." **The task is not to impose learning, but to lead learning out from resourceful unconscious minds filled with the memories of wanted and unwanted outcomes.** Many approaches to learning stop too early and do not utilize brain-compatible learning environments to encourage students to use their *unconscious* minds that hold what is waiting to be expressed beyond the mere awareness of information.

- During childhood lots of learning occurs that is beyond awareness. Learning should always be the most natural and entertaining activity that adults and children experience. **No emotional unpleasantness allowed!** (Emotions are at the center of everything we do or don't do, including learning.)

- Criticism, no matter how well intended, is never as supportive or productive as positive, patient encouragement. **The put-downs and negative evaluations, too often found in traditional teaching, work against optimal learning experiences.** Instead of griping about the current situation or outcome, consider how things might be different. Self-initiated positive behavior can build the necessary conceptual base for what *to-do*, not what to-fix when learning.
- High expectations are valuable, but they should not be confused with specific outcome goals and predetermined milestones. Find challenges that lead to growth and eventually to the individual's full potential and capability. Outcome-goals tend to be specific; process-goals involve staying in the present. **Avoid outcome-goals, while using process-goals!**
- When providing new information or reviewing past experiences, meaningful approaches to learning encourage and reinforce the students' belief in their childhood capacity to learn and succeed. The emotion of fear must be banished from approaches to learning and replaced with **constant emotional support of the students' self-worth.**
- As far back as the 1950s, Georgi Lozanov and other researchers came to recognize and believe that everyone had the potential to learn at a rate two to five times faster than the present education system considered normal. **They also believed that even that rate of learning could be improved upon.**

Lozanov proposed learning environments be childlike play-rooms, where providers of information take on a nurturing role, reinforcing the learner's own attempts to learn with positive responses. Downplaying and looking past unwanted outcomes and seeing them as useful attempts, is a component of integrative learning.

Lozanov called this approach "suggestopedia." This implies *general* suggestions (not *how-to* directions) are the cornerstone of information delivery systems. This approach points to self-actualization and success orientation (not fixing). Humans are not wired to fail tests, miss golf shots, or have car accidents; we are all wired for survival. (The romantic stage of learning.)

The brain might say, **"Give me the right set of suggestions (not directions) and get me to believe them, and I can learn anything!"**

When the conditions that favor meaningful learning are understood, individuals learn faster and with more depth of reasoning than they had previously believed possible. Before a teacher can successfully stimulate learning and growth in others, it helps them to have insights into the nature of learning. **If you have been brought up in a culture that believes learning is difficult, you may have been sold a bill of goods.**

Many traditional approaches to learning have misled students by doing most of the thinking for them. After depriving students of fruitful opportunities to use their brains, we complain that they do not know how to think or problem solve. The aim, of course, is to help students to become independent learners one day. Telling students how to do things not only insults their intelligence, it can also create confusion. **Help students learn how to learn, don't give them answers.**

The poet, Robert Frost, put it this way, "A student is someone who is somewhere and trying to get somewhere else." To support this insight, students should first be given the big concept or full picture of the subject and then later any details will fall into place. **Starting with details is not brain-compatible for learning.**

What Constitutes Meaningful Learning?

"Assist individuals in becoming self-sustaining long-term learners." **John D. Bransford**

There are books about learning methodology written for an audience that include educators, parents, employers, coaches, designers of curriculum, instructors, business training instructors, etc. There are also books on the same topic written for individuals who are trying to learn. This book was written to contribute to a basic understanding of the nature of learning and assist both groups in becoming "self-sustaining, life-long learners" (to use the words of John D. Bransford).

Two descriptions of meaningful learning are 1) creating the skills that can create more skills and 2) creating the capacity to create more capacity. This is the kind of learning that supports more new learning. Just knowing a piece of information would be a very small measure of the quality of learning that has taken place.

Meaningful Learning improves learning potential, it is also:

Joyful and fulfilling	Open-ended and direct
Personal and satisfying	Flexible and portable
Adventurous and safe	Inventive and personal
Interesting and challenging	Internal and democratic
Autobiographical and stimulating	Plain spoken and tinkering
Unconscious and lasting	Wordless and seeing
Indirect and spontaneous	Visionary and felt

An example that *meaningful-learning* had been encoded[41] would be after an individual learns content and they can also put it

---

[41] Boyorie 1994

to use in a variety of environments that are different from the one in which the content was first learned. Approaches to learning with the aim of meaningful long-term improvement are less about avoiding, reacting to, or overcoming unwanted outcomes and more about being proactive about learning what needs to be accomplished. Proactive approaches aim at what to do and not at following how-to directions from a perceived expert to fix unwanted outcomes.

Meaningful learning takes place when information develops into personal know-how knowledge for use in ever-changing environments. It is fair to say that in an ever-changing environment information does not become knowledge until it can be put to use unconsciously. New York University Professor Joseph E. LeDoux Ph.D states, "Conscious recognition of unconscious learning is meaningful learning."

Meaningful Learning:
- Prepares individuals for future learning (Weimer 2005)
- Creates the ability to use information after significant periods of disuse (Bjork 1994)

> *"The goal of education is better conceived as students develop the tools and strategies needed to acquire the knowledge necessary to think productively. The meaning of knowledge has shifted from being able to remember and repeat information to being able to find and use it."*
> Nobel Laureate Herbert Simon (1996)

Meaningful learning develops the tools to hear what is not being said; to see what is not being shown, to read between the lines and to have answers for questions yet to be asked.

A meaningful approach to learning is focusing on changing insights that individuals currently have (not unwanted outcomes), so they can change unwanted outcomes on their own.

Meaningful learning does not appear to be a composed result, but an outcome brought on by spontaneous interaction in ever-changing conditions.

Meaningful learning is a reflection of how ever-changing environments require a fresh random application of basics. It is meaningful learning when our basic understanding can be used in many ways under the influence of the past experiences that exist in our unconscious mind.

- Meaningful learning is accomplished by more than accurate subject content, which is only one side of the story
- Meaningful learning is about what can be accomplished and not about overcoming an unwanted outcome
- Meaningful learning is a product of the brain's ability to filter new information through the lens of prior knowledge and prior experiences (both wanted and unwanted outcomes), giving personal meaning to information

To struggle is an imperative of meaningful learning. *"Desirable Developmental Difficulties"* is how Harvard's Graduate School of Education refers to struggles and unwanted outcomes. Unwanted outcomes are more valuable than wanted outcomes when learning because they can provide useful feedback for future reference.

Personal innovation is the engine of meaningful learning. When approaches to learning create an environment that fails to promote innovation on the part of a student, this would be like trying to make a car lighter by removing its engine.

Brain-compatible learning environments promote sitting back, relaxing and letting insights from the non-conscious mind handle most of it. You can have external peace of mind while the brain is actively engaged in non-consciously joining insights from past experiences with what is taking place in the present.

"The mind is a wonderful, sense making device that takes confusing information and unconsciously simplifies it according to the rule of thumb," states Arron M. Sackett, (Psychologist, University of St. Thomas, MN)

The Non-conscious Mind

"The state of least excitation of consciousness is the field of all possibilities."
Mahesh Yogi

Researchers Konrad Z. Lorenz and Niko Tinbergen point out that, "We learn by nature (a survival skill) and not by reason and without conscious thought. Learning is a reflex, an involuntary form of survival. It's a non-conscious pattern of behavior that is responding to environmental stimuli. Learning is an innate capability impelled from within."

There are two levels of the mind, one is non-conscious, the other conscious. The non-conscious can be more important than the conscious for guiding what we do. The non-conscious is filled with the raw material of past experiences that influences our reasoning, learning and decisions. The conscious mind has no record of past experiences and can only process less than fifty bits of information per second, while the non-conscious mind can process millions of bits in the same time frame.

Joseph LeDoux, Ph.D New York University said, "Most cognitive processes have been found to occur non-consciously, with only the end product reaching the conscious mind if at all. Contrary to popular belief, a cognitive process involves a non-conscious processing mechanism."[42] Noam Chomsky, Darwin, Steven Pinker and others have also pointed to the idea that learning is a natural and instinctive tendency. When we go to the movies, or read a book and then tell our friends the story, did we try to learn that information? No! In a stress free brain-compatible learning environment, learning takes place without consciously trying to learn.

Students who experience meaningful learning do not simply remember what they are told. They construct their own meaning and understanding based on their past experiences; a nonconscious process that we are unaware is taking place. This reality is why stories and metaphors are important in learning environments.

I can be aware that I am in a place, but everything I see, hear, taste, feel, or smell, is evaluated unconsciously by prior knowledge.

All new learning is based on a transfer of information from the context of previous experiences. People use what they already know to construct new learning and new understandings (unconsciously). When what we know and believe is a misconception, meaningful learning can be suppressed. The same holds true if new learning is misinterpreted because of prior knowledge.[43]

Without carefully considering the knowledge that individuals already bring to a learning situation, it is difficult to evaluate what they will understand about new learning. New learning is an unconscious blend of old and new information.

David Eagleman, a neuroscientist at Baylor College of Medicine points out that only a tiny five to ten percent fraction of our brain is dedicated to conscious behavior. It is the unconscious

---

[42] *Human*, by Michael S. Gazzaniga, p. 67

[43] *How People Learn*, by Committee on Developments in the Science of Learning with additional material from the Committee on Learning Research and Educational Practice and National Research Council (Sep 15, 2000), p. 68

workings of the brain that are crucial to are everyday functioning including learning.

In his book *Incognito,* David Eagleman notes that there is a gap between the amount of information the brain consciously knows and what your unconscious mind is actually capable of accessing. We are not aware of the vast majority of the brain's ongoing non-conscious activities, nor would we want to be. If we were, that would interfere with the brain's highly efficient capabilities for learning and performing.

We could say that the brain secretly performs an enormous amount of work incognito. Eagleman notes that, "The best way to mess up playing the piano; or get out of breath; or miss a golf shot is to consciously analyze what you are doing." [44]

Eagleman points out that there is a difference between knowledge and awareness. Implicit memory is completely separate from explicit memory. Implicitly learned information (non-consciously) is simply not accessible on command to consciousness (it shows up when needed). Unconscious learning and most everything about our interactions with the world rests on this reality. Ah-ha moments do not come on command – they just arrive.

One of the most impressive features of our brain is its flexibility for learning almost anything that comes its way. Our non-conscious implicit flexibility accounts for a large part of our learning, or what is consider human intelligence, as the brain is unconsciously fashioning neural connections to match the "task at hand," unconsciously.

In the late 1800s, Hermann Ebbinghaus wrote, "most experiences remain concealed from consciousness and yet they produce an effect which is significant, which indicates their previous existence." The best reason we have for believing that unconscious learning exists is that we have all experienced it.

---

[44] *Discovery Magazine,* September 2011, "Secret Life of the Mind" p. 51

The Non-Conscious Learner

- **The Brain is:** A behind the scenes thinker, a laboratory with a view from the inside
- **The Brain is:** Taking advantage of earlier interactions with a gradual, agile, evolutionary approach
- **The Brain** uses reverse engineering (adapting), with the experimental features of slow and steady developmental interactions
- **The Brain** incrementally develops continuous improvements

That a master of anything was first a master of learning is an accurate description of the human brain.

Efficient approaches to learning take advantage of every individual's ability to learn non-consciously, based on our past experiences.

A "just for the fun of it" approach, guided by little more than some basic and practical advice, often brings out the best individuals have to offer when it comes to meaningful learning.

University of Cambridge Professor Theresa Marteau said, "More emphasis on strategies that target our automatic brain processes is needed." She quotes William James from a book he wrote in 1899, "Ninety-nine or possibly ninety-nine and ninety-nine thousandths of our activity is purely automatic and habitual from our rising in the morning to our lying down each night."

In brain-compatible learning environments, students are not seen as a canvas to be written on; rather they are seen more like a sponge that can release what it's holding. It's always springtime in the brain, as new information and past experiences are growing together.

For over two decades there has been a new phase of re-thinking emerging from science that can move individuals (givers and receivers of information) closer to relying on the process of non-conscious natural learning; which is at the core of a human be-ings' basic survival skills.

Meaningful learning is exciting, entertaining, and romantic. Everyone *loves* to learn and the *excitement* of making progress is leveraged by how *entertaining* it can be, especially if the entertain-ment is from the self-discovery.

> During meaningful learning, principles from the nature of learn-ing, in the form of unconscious acts of self-assessment and self-adjustments, connect individuals with their environment.
> **This formula of unconscious assessment is the underbelly of human development and growth.**

"All our outward behavior is a result of neurological (in-ternal) processing patterns. If a neurological pattern does not oc-cur, then the behavior does not occur."
Miller, Galanter, and Pribram
Play with these insights about meaningful learning:

- *"What human beings do best is learn. The human brain seems perfectly designed for learning."*[45]
- *"Once an individual being is born, it starts to learn for it-self."*[46]
- *"The growth of intelligence is never a conscious process. Change always takes place below awareness."*[47]

[45] *Brain Facts*, by Eric Jensen, p. 25
[46] *How the Brain Learns*, by John McCain, p. 18
[47] *Magical Child*, p. 141

The views given here are based on mankind's natural gift for learning without consciously trying to learn. ***"Everyone is born a genius,"*** said R. Buckminster Fuller.[48]

Again, human beings are conceived and come into the world with the ability to instantaneously and simultaneously be an efficient self-learner and then an efficient self-teacher (i.e.: after we learn something is dangerous, we then teach ourselves to stay away).

NOTES:

_____

_____

_____

_____

_____

_____

_____

_____

_____

_____

_____

_____

_____

_____

_____

_____

_____

_____

[48] *The Birth of The Mind* by Gary Marcus, p. 15

Part Five

Strategies

"Students are only learning disabled in some learning environments."
David Rose, Harvard Graduate School of Education

The nature of natural learning is at war against too much of everything. A reality that comes to life in the nature of learning is that big moments are not always in the script.

There are **strategies** and approaches that support personal innovation, self-reliance and long-term learning. Some **strategies** for finding points of entry for modernizing learning include:

- Attention on what to do, not how to do it or fixing unworkable outcomes. Learning is based more heavily on unworkable outcomes that are not criticized or judged, than on workable outcomes.
- Create safe non-judgmental learning environments.
- See all outcomes (including unworkable) as feedback for future reference, not as failure. (Failure = <u>F</u>inding <u>A</u>ccess <u>I</u>nto <u>L</u>earning, <u>U</u>ncovering <u>R</u>elevant <u>E</u>ducation).
- Students do not need evaluators – they need a guided search for solutions. Use smart approaches that realize no student is broken or in need of fixing. (On a journey of learning and developing, the present outcomes have nothing missing, they are just developing.)
- Use a play-to-learn approach. (When incorporating new learning use a playful, random approach.) Help people invent their own skills.

Giving students choices can be more useful than giving those directions or corrections. (Do you like "A", "B", or "C"?)

- Let learning be an autobiographical process that promotes self-discovery and self-assessment.
- Learning will be more efficient when how-to directions are avoided.
- The use of broad, general concepts and metaphors can be more useful than using detailed information. The brain can use a general, just in-the-ball-park concept. Help individuals understand general concepts. The brain just wants the gist of things.

- Promote self-regulation; make students feel "smart" by developing their self-reliance skills.

Questions that can enhance thinking, seeing options, creativity and learning include:
- How would you have done it?
- What may happen next?
- What do you believe was the cause?
- What would be the best choice?
- What would you do next?
- What has been left out?
- What are the different ways to use this?
- What would modify this?
- What is the most important element?
- What is the difference between A and B?
- What is this similar to?

Also ask students to:
- Find more than one example to support evidence or views.
- Find strengths and weakness about a point of view.
- Find ways to compare and contrast strengths in different context.
- Find more than one source or a variety of perspectives on a particular idea.

Developing Skills

The nature of learning is less about acts of "in-struction" and more about "out-struction" and drawing out what the student knows, so they can learn more.

Adapted from Bill Marvin insights (A business management consultant).

Some models of management are closer to a law enforcement approach than to anything else. "Find things that are wrong and fix them!" This is fine if you want to spend your life looking for things that are wrong. However, there is a more productive way to make progress.

I think the model we need to adopt is an efficient coaching model. It looks for strengths. Efficient coaching looks at the talent. Coaches should say, "You are doing well in this area, now this is the next thing we need to work on." They help bring out natural talent and measure their own success by the success achieved by their players.

Efficient coaching is an inside-out education, where the players see their own answers. In contrast, what we saw in many schools was outside-in education where the right answers were held by the teacher. To improve coaching skills, get good at asking questions. Great coaches ask insightful, probing questions that cause their players to think. It is hard to get yourself in trouble if you are either asking or answering questions. It is only when approaches to learning make statements (preaching or lecturing) that dangerous ground is tread upon.

Notes from reading *Teaching for Understanding*, edited by Martha Stone Wisk:

Richard Meyer, "*Conceptual models* promote understanding and solving problems more flexibly than when students do not develop a *conceptual model*."

You can have a mental model of anything without understanding it. Mental models involve a certain point of view and while they are informed, they can also be misleading.

Conceptual models avoid this contradiction.

Conceptual models explain, justify, relate, extrapolate and apply information in ways that go beyond one's knowledge and routine skills.

Conceptual models can be simple but rich with implications that support thinking and acting flexibly with what one knows, much like a jazz musician.

How ideas, process, relationships, patterns and questions are investigated, leads to the quality of *conceptual models*.

Subject matter is the sub-goal, with *conceptual models* supporting the process of learning and performing the main goal.

When learning is approached through a range of entry points, from various topic perspectives, while using a variety of learning materials and resources, *conceptual models* can be developed.

The framework for teaching for understanding is almost as old as human history. Parables and metaphors that make connections with students' various worlds have been used by teachers going back before Plato's time. These stories construct concept images that go to understanding.

A student's current understanding of himself/herself and the circumstances supports new learning.

Teaching for understanding has the view that what receivers of information are learning needs to be used in many different circumstances in and out of the organized learning environment, thereby serving as a base for ongoing and extended learning that is always alive with possibilities.

John Frederick Herbarts suggested that each stage of new learning had to be integrated with past learning, while looking for entry points that connected with current knowledge. This view was similar to Alfred North Whitehead's ideas of a continuous learning cycle.

When something has been learned, normally it can be demonstrated, what may be less clear is what made that kind of meaningful learning possible (i.e. a brain-compatible approach).

Many pieces of the puzzle fell into place when research revealed the brain's connection to learning. In the past it is fair to say that many, who were interested in the topic of learning, relied more on traditional views than on sound studies and respected research about:

- What learning is
- How learning happens
- How learning can last

Michael S. Gazzaniga, one of the world's leading neuroscientists, author of *Human* wrote, "We humans are special. All of us can solve problems effortlessly (i.e. learn effortlessly). Humans have the ability to reflect on their own thoughts which is called <u>metacognition</u>, a component of human existence while interacting with the environment."

"If the nature of learning were to make only one suggestion to humans for enhancing the results from acts of learning it may be to "make the approach to learning brain-compatible."
Teaching for Understanding

Receivers of information should understand:

- Their present ideas and feelings influence learning
- Learning is a multi-step non-linear process
- Learning plays a significant role in all of our lives
- Learning compares and makes decisions about what to keep or reject
- Learning can be approached in such a way that it can empowers individuals
- Learning for understanding includes comprehension, design, enactment and integration

For example, find key elements that receivers of information can <u>comprehend</u> and relate to. <u>Design</u> the curriculum on these key elements. Use an approach to learning that causes receivers of information to <u>enact</u> the key elements of the topic. <u>Integrate</u> these key elements with prior knowledge and experiences.

- Learning for understanding relates directly to insights about process goals.
- Develop and apply opportunities for understanding, while avoiding criticism.
- Promote and engage multiple expressions of learning in different contexts.
- Create reflective engagement in challenging, approachable tasks.
- Provide opportunities for receivers of information to demonstrate their understanding.
- Use implicit insights that move beyond explicit descriptions.
- Meaningful learning produces flexible knowledge and portable skills, and not just one view (a reflection of learning for understanding).

What follows was adapted from *Teaching Today* by Geoff Petty:

Professors John Hattie's and Robert Margorno's research, along with other studies have demonstrated that Cognitive and Constructivist approaches appear to be the most efficient paths to meaningful learning.

Principles to cognitive approaches to learning include:

- Use higher order skills, including planning.
- Use high order tasks requiring analysis, evolution and synthesis.
- Use laddered tasks that go from simple and concrete, from obvious to more abstract.

Principles of constructivist approaches to learning include:

- Using approaches that require students to create and apply their own ideas, in order to decide what to do.

- Using approaches that support what the student is doing can be more important than what a provider of information does. Acts of teaching are just a means to the end, it is learning that counts.
- Use a trial and error approach to learning that requires students to evaluate their own workable and unworkable outcomes (valuable feedback for future reference).
- Create students' participation that makes acts of learning interesting.
- Keep in mind that learning is grounded in acts of doing in safe emotional environments.

Common Cognitivist and Constructivist Learning Strategies Include:

- Asking questions and guiding discovery.
- The use of poor outcomes to explore learning from misunderstandings.
- Have receivers of information identify key parts and how they relate to the whole.
- Have receivers of information discuss the material to be learned and construct insights that are personal in nature.
-

"The ultimate goal of the education system is to shift the burden of pursuing their own education to the student."
J.W. Gardner

Teaching for understanding has a framework that puts attention on what students do, rather than on what teachers do. Understanding grows by performing one's current knowledge. Let's define understanding as "going beyond the information given" to extend, synthesize, apply, or otherwise use what one knows in creative ways. This extension includes (but is not limited to) exploring, interpreting, analyzing, relating, comparing and making analogies.

Have appropriate tools to utilize a full spectrum of intelligence and perform in myriad creative ways aids understanding. Instead of rehearsing or recreating what others have done, true understanding engages learners in creating their own insights, which they can then; incorporate into their own autobiography.

Insights from How People Learn

- Begin with the student's questions rather than with a fixed curriculum. (p. 157)
- Topic knowledge without knowledge of how individuals learn and how to guide the processes of learning would not yield meaningful learning. (p. 157)
- A change in models of efficient learning is needed from what many teachers, parents and students currently model. (p. 141)
- Expose students to the major frustrations of the topic to be learned. (p. 139)
- Engage students in cognitive conflicts, and then have discussions about conflicting viewpoints. Piaget 1973
- A major goal of education is to prepare students for flexible adoptions to new problems and settings. Time spent learning for understanding has different consequences for transfer, than time spent learning facts. (p. 77)
- Rather than focus on specific solutions, highlight the general features of an action or critical decision. (White and Fredrickson, 1998)
- Have students use self-assessment. (p. 140)

The Notion of How
Kapil Gupta *Siddha Performance*

- The world is in love with the notion of *how*. Students love to ask for it. Teachers love to dispense it. But the student who asks this is not a true seeker. And the teacher who dispenses it is not a true teacher.
- Why?
- Because *how* asks for a prescription.
- *How* asks for a method.
- *How* asks for a template.
- *How* asks for a recipe.
- *How* asks for *THE WAY*.
- And those who ask the *how* question, ask the question precisely because they are ready to follow the *how* answer.
- And if a person is willing to follow the way indicated by another it is only because he believes that there is, in fact, a path that is ready for him to tread. He has not yet come to the realization that a path is not a road, but an experience.
- And that experience is not something to join or walk toward. It is something that is continually and incrementally unfolding before him as a function of his way of perceiving his place in the world.
- In some ways, the very act of teaching is to misunderstand and to underestimate the nature of the human machine. As teaching is largely about the dispensation of information. The human brain does not respond to another's words. It responds to its perception and translation of those words. In this way, the teacher and the student are forever speaking a different language.
- The teacher teaches the *how*, not only because he feels it is the only way or the best way. But because he simply loves to do so. He gains something from it. Emotionally and financially.

- The student asks the *how*, because he seeks a quick resolution to his problem. And though it may only work temporarily, he becomes accustomed to this chase.
- The true seeker is consumed with the what. For him, the *how* is like the remora fish that rides the belly of the great shark.
- The great teachers are not teachers at all. They are seekers. They are not so much interested in their student's development of technique, as they are in the development of his understanding.
- Teaching technique will lead to an enhancement of one's technique. But never to the realization of one's potential.
- Asking for the *how* does not make one great. It makes one dependent.
- Seek understanding. Not instruction. For the ultimate technique is devoid of conscious action. And the ultimate understanding is devoid of thought.

NOTES:

_____

_____

_____

_____

_____

_____

_____

_____

_____

_____

_____

Studies

"Investigating assumptions gives the opportunity to evaluate their value."
Author Unknown

Caine and Caine

Renate and Geoffrey Caine traveled all over the United States and asked questions of many people when conducting research for their book. They point out that mental models shape our day-to-day decisions and interactions and these models are often deeply ingrained with assumptions and generalizations that are inaccurate. Mental models are the way we perceive the world and make sense of it. These fundamental beliefs are powerful because they will help organize experiences, information and strategies. In doing research for their book the answers the Caines received invariably reflected some of the finest thinking of our time. They heard "<u>Learning</u> is change in thinking and behavior due to new understanding", "<u>Teaching</u> is giving learners the opportunity to do their own best learning" and "<u>School</u> is anywhere this can happen and it doesn't have to be a classroom."

The kind of brain-based research that the Caines used to gain an understanding was quantitative, participative and dynamic, as are all the studies and research compiled here. The Caines said, "We observed, collected data, asked questions, searched for answers, read profusely, modified and expanded assumptions connected to our knowledge, and then we would start all over again. This is the same process, we should add, that we sought to induce in the people with whom we worked."[49]

---

[49] p. 23

The Caines research led them to a summary of three instructional approaches, with approach # 3 being the most efficient in their view.

Approach 1. This approach relies on top down thinking and the control of information and facts to be disseminated by teachers. A stand and deliver method.

Approach 2. Is still primarily a command and control mode of instruction, but it's organized around concepts rather than just memorizing, with an eye to creating meaning.

Approach 3. Differs radically from approaches #1 and #2, because it's much more learner centered (from bottom to top). This kind of instruction is more fluid and open. It includes elements of self-organization as students had purposeful projects, critical ideas and meaningful questions, within a context of educational experiences that approach the complexity of real life.

Arizona State University

It was an honor for me to be invited by Dr. Debbie Crews to speak during the World Scientific Conference at Arizona State University, March 2001. The aim of this prestigious conference was to influence and improve learning in the future. What scientists and educators from all over the world presented about teaching and learning that week was relevant for learning anything. To be in the company of these men and women was invaluable. Some of the research presented at this gathering included the following:

Random Training supports long-term retention of skills more efficiently than drills and rigid blueprints. It enhances learning to change environments frequently.

Self-learning, or education by selection, or choice, is more effective for long-term retention than following directions.

A learning model that is general in nature is more effective for retention of skills than a specific expert model. Models that are just in-the-ball-park lead students in the direction of highly skilled results more efficiently than expert models that are better used as inspirations to motivate.

Efficient Learning Environments: 1) Pay attention to the learner, not poor habits, 2) help learners discover what's needed 3) provide learners with the opportunity to personalize information and develop the tools of adapting (reverse engineering).

A number of factors that can fragment learning were discussed during the conference at Arizona State including: stress, rigid systems, drills, rote learning, expert models, lack of core knowledge, little or no creative play, little sensory stimulation, little opportunity for developing imagination, few chances to solve problems and training in a get-it or did not get-it environment.

Columbia University

Columbia University's Dr. Bailey points out in *Working Knowledge, Work-Based Learning and Education Reform* that today cognitive scientists are drawing on a wide range of sources including some nineteenth century educational thinkers to add to their own discoveries about how people learn. For example, in 1875 Francis Parker replaced a traditional teaching curriculum with educational projects and learning experiences that were meaningful to students in schools in Quincy, Massachusetts.

One of America's first great thinkers about education and founder of progressive education in the United States, John Dewey, built on Francis Packer's insights about learning. **Dewey saw traditional education as being isolated from reality and passive in its methods.** The approaches to learning for schools that Dewey founded at the University of Chicago had three principles (Farnham – Diggory, 1990)

#1. Instruction must focus on the development of the student's mind, not on blocks of subject matter.

#2. Instruction must be integrated into project-oriented approaches.

#3. The progression through years of school education must go from practical experiences, to formal information, to integrated studies.

Dr. Bailey also points out that John Dewey's principles required students to make observations and predictions, thus developing the student's own scientific skills. In terms of designing efficient learning environments Dewey left us some key ideas:

- The student is the center of learning.
- Learning is an active engagement, with an environment structured for education (not test scores).
- Integration of mind and action, head and hand, academic and vocation, promotes learning. (Branford, Stein, Arbitman – Smith and Vye 1985); in 1989 Pea said, "The student is a spectacular learner," pointing out:
    - Learning takes place in context (real world situations), with immediate feedback on the outcome of the student's actions available
    - Learning is guided, providing structure for connections between every experience.
    - Learning in context gives students insights about the role of information in problem solving. Drills often are not in context; copying expert models is following, which is a lower brain activity and not problem solving. Concepts and skills are acquired as tools, with a range of problem solving purposes for enhancing flexible knowledge and portable skills.

Dr. Bailey and others talked about the value of apprenticeships, and I will paraphrase some of these studies. Traditional apprenticeship programs in the 19th century were a source of ideas, promoting efficient learning environments for how individuals learned (Lave 1993, Jordan 1987, Screbnor and Sach's 1990).

Spending time in apprentice programs is not so much practicing for the real thing, as it was doing many useful and necessary tasks. Apprentices are driven by the work to be accomplished (not how-to information). Apprenticeships should not be recognized as a conscious learning effort at all. Much of what an apprentice does is difficult to differentiate from "*play.*" Traditional apprenticeship programs use apprentices for trial runs and practice, where schools tend to be a practice of specification (Lave, 1988).

> During apprenticeships - the evolution of a learner's competence emerges naturally and continuously in the context of work and is evaluated by what is being accomplished, rather than from a test.

"The success or failure of a task that has been performed is normally obvious and needs no commentary. To a large extent the person who judges the apprentice performance is the apprentice himself or herself - rather than the expert"
Dr. Bailey

After the apprentice is aware of core knowledge, they know what remains to be learned. The ability to move on to the next skill is largely under the influence of the apprentice rather than the master. In other words, the apprentice tends to own the problems of learning and is in charge of moving on to the next skill. **During an apprenticeship, whatever instruction the apprentice receives, it originates not from a teacher doing teaching, but from the learner doing, observing and adjusting.**

Traditional apprenticeships show what efficient context-led learning looks like. Cognitive science has developed *analogies* appropriate for learning through the apprenticeship approach based on playful self-discovery. When students are being told *how-to* do something, it's a violent change from nature's plan for self-development with external learning influences that should be avoided at all costs.

Efficient approaches to learning could easily be called interactive brain-on, hands-on entertainment, as students invent their own style or skills and develop their own information base, (or what is referred to as their own working knowledge).

Mankind's brain is designed to distill, translate and interpret, not passively follow directions. Joseph Clinton Pearce described this design as a "two-way flow of assimilation and accommodation."

Ten Insights About Learning

Based on studies by Chris Johnson, Head Coach, Sutton Coldfield Tennis

1. **Spaced Practice:** Train little (small sessions) and often.[50]
2. **Cognitive Overload:** Reduce information; simplify to prevent cognitive overload.
3. **Chunking:** Create a single idea or thought that represent several components.
4. **Order:** Present information in a pattern that leads to meaning.
5. **Episodic and Systematic Memory:** There is memory for procedure and memory for facts. Thinking about facts can

---

[50] The Spacing Effect 1988 Case Study regarding the failure to apply.

slow down learning procedures. We cannot do both effectively at the same time.

6. **Psychological Attention**: Keep in mind that the emotional state of the learning environment influences learning. Learning environments must be emotionally safe.

7. **Context:** When learning happens it occurs in the sequence the content is going to be learned in.

8. **Learning by Doing:** William James and John Dewey promoted Active Learning over Theory Explanation.

9. **Understanding Pier Groups:** "We underestimate the influence of pier groups and genetics. Judith Harris, *The Nature of Assumption.*

10. **Myths:** Discard snake-oil learning style techniques and focus on the cause content. The entire brain is involved when learning.

Some Thoughts On Good Brains but Poor Learning

Everyone who comes into the world with a healthy brain has been predisposed to be a competent, natural learner. Learning is a survival skill that we are all born with; why then does poor learning even exist? How can the most efficient learning machine we know of, the brain, take part in poor learning?

The brain is a genetic inheritance passed on over time. It is a biological organ that changes automatically and unconsciously. Our daily functions, dysfunctions, and thoughts cause these ongoing internal adjustments in our brain's wiring. Learning is about experiences and the outcome of those experiences. Unconscious *implicit* learning is our main form of meaningful learning. On the other hand, explicit approaches to learning can be the poorest form of learning.

All systems in the brain learn unconsciously. Fortunately, what we learn unconsciously can be used consciously. Meaningful long-term learning is supported by conscious recognition of unconscious learning; for example those wonderful "ah – ha" moments of conscious recognition.

Most of the brain is engaged when we are learning. All brain components take part; genes; cells; synapse; neurons; subsystems; and networks. Even in the 21st century, like all other elements of time and evaluation, the brain is still a work in progress. As the environment changes, the brain keeps adapting.

Emotions

If approaches to learning expect to be efficient they must accept the strong relationship between cognitive function and emotions. The emotional consequences of our interactions are often overlooked in learning environments, thereby causing less than optimal outcomes.

When we are learning the body, mind, and the brain come together emotionally. Birds fly, fishes swim, and people feel.

We have emotions that bring attention to, or away from what we are learning. The emotions of fear and stress are mostly involuntary unconscious reactions based on past experiences. Fear and stress can hurt learning and performing.

Mary Helen Immordino Yang, Ed.D, a leading research scientist in the field of how learning is influenced by emotions, states, "The way we feel influences how we are learning in every learning environment. We attach feels to things and things to feels. We always feel something that pushes us on, or away from what we are learning." Meaningful learning environments are emotionally safe and void of negative judgments of outcomes.

Play

Approaches to learning create emotionally safe, learning environments that are playful in their approach toward making students feel smart. **Perhaps the main responsibility of any provider of information is to make receivers of information feel smart.**

When people feel smart they take the kind of risks and struggles that learning is founded on. All play is practice for life. It is a universal instinct that promotes interest in learning. Play is indirect preparation for future learning.

If something has been playfully learned in one context, it is an act of indirect preparation for learning and applying something new in a different context. New learning happens on the shoulders of the indirect preparation that prior learning provided, as good brains support meaningful learning.

The personal perceptions that both providers and receivers of information have about learning, emotions and the culture of approaches to learning will influence whether meaningful learning is even possible. Many providers of information have been referred to as good communicators.

What is the value of what they are sharing? How are they sharing what they know?

Poor communication is a problem causing discord between people; countries; businesses; parents and children; teachers and students; and employer and employees. Where should we start to find solutions for any miscommunication?

The brain is the gateway to learning. When providers and receivers of information have insights into the brain's connections to this process of change, the design of their approaches for learning becomes more in-line with the nature of learning.

Brain-compatible approaches to learning are very simple; to help individuals enhance their ability to learn anything. I would put it this way; in learning environments how approaches to learning are going to be designed will be addressed first, followed by the subject of choice. The nature of learning has an unconscious mix of challenges and struggles that are wrapped in curiosity, based on past experiences and prior knowledge. Struggling is very important when learning, points out, Professor Robert Bjork head of UCLA's learning and forgetting lab.

Keeping students curious may be the best form of motivation as they ask, *"what's next?"* **or** *"What else can I do with this?"*

We can do things for hours without realizing how much time we have spent. Is it motivation or curiosity that leads to losing one's self in a task? What's on the next page? Curiosity that leads to motivation. My suggestion, keep students curious and they will stay motivated. What is this or that? How can I do this or that? In my view it is curiosity the supports motivation.

Touched by shades of time, the subtle tones of past experiences are reborn when joined with insights that are coming from interest in what is going on in the now.

The brain operates by consciously and unconsciously gathering elements and reorganizing them into a cohesive whole. It could be said that the brain is always taking a class and is making notes about the patterns and sequences of information that make sense and have meaning for future reference, based on past experiences. The brain's classroom is the environment where life's interactions take place.

When the "language of learning" is brain-compatible it often has long breaks between personal insights that arrive from the inventory of information and personal perceptions encoded in the unconscious mind. There are those times when mentally walking away; not focusing; or giving the brain some breathing room brings on a new or different view enveloped in a rush of adrenaline release. This opens a pathway for developing meaningful learning that is personal and autobiographical in nature.

Focus is not as useful as attention. It has been shown that focusing can slow down creativity, memory, and problem solving skills. This is why we remember the answer after we leave the test. Pay attention; just let information flow in or out of the brain. Trying to focus is not a component of the nature of learning; attention is.

Meaningful learning is dragged down when students are hearing about "what is wrong" and demands that what's wrong needs to be fixed. Freedom from a prison of judgment and criticism that some approaches to learning provide is the aim of information delivery systems.

To Focus or Not?

Read this section with two realities in mind; 1) past experiences and prior knowledge influence what we can learn, perform and create; 2) and information from many different locations in the brain will unconsciously come together to help solve problems.

Research by neuroscientists from Harvard and the University of Toronto found that acts of *focusing* can be damaging to learning and performing. Decisions not to focus, or the inability to focus (ADHD), help to ensure a richer mixture of creative thoughts than focusing can produce.

Martha Farah, Ph.D, University of Pennsylvania neuroscientist, "People assume that increased focus is always better, but they do not realize that intense focus comes with real trade-offs, and any big insights are not going to happen."

When individuals are *not* filtering out the world by trying to focus, they end up unconsciously letting in useful information. This occurs without a **focused, predictable perspective,** as the brain unconsciously considers all sorts of analogies that provide useful insights for learning and solving problems.

Prof. Jordan Peterson, University of Toronto neuroscientist, "Without focusing, creativity remains in contact with information that is constantly streaming to the brain from the environment."

Dr. Marcus Raichle, Washington University, neurologist, "When your brain is supposedly doing nothing (not focusing) it is really doing a tremendous amount."

"Creativity is the result of time wasted."
Albert Einstein

MRI studies by Raichle demonstrated that during non-focusing, or what he calls "a default stage," there was elaborate electrical conversation going on between the front and back parts of the brain. "I knew that there must be good reason for all this neural activity, I just didn't know what the reason was." Why was the brain so active during non-focusing or daydreaming? This was the question Raichle asked about a lazy mental process and found the brain was very active during this stage.

He found that the brain's prefrontal folds fall in sync with the posterior cingulated medial temporal precuneus. These brain areas normally do not interact directly. It is when daydreaming without focus that these areas of the brain begin to work closely with each other, for the purpose of making unconscious associations by connecting new experiences with prior experiences.

In our non-focusing stage, the brain has the ability to blend together different kinds of skills and concepts that are encoded in different locations in the brain, and can notice what would be overlooked during conscious focus.

Studies show that instead of responding completely to the outside world, that during non-focusing the brain will start to explore its *inner* database, searching for relationships in a more relaxed fashion. This relaxed mental process often runs parallel with increased activity in the brain's less linear and more creative right hemisphere.

The brain's ability to blend together skills and concepts that are not the same and are encoded in different locations in the brain reduces what would be overlooked if one were consciously focusing. There is an advantage of knowing that insight comes from our environment and this can make it easier to have insights that support learning and performing.

> **Suggestion:** **Stop trying so hard to focus and let insights just arrive from you non-conscious mind.**

In a relaxed state of mind, it is more likely that the brain's light of attention will look *inward,* in the direction of unconsciously connecting dissimilar information. **When we are diligently focused, our attention tends to be directed *outward,* in the direction of the details of the problem we are trying to solve.** This outward attention actually *prevents* us from making the kind of connections in the brain that lead to workable insights. It is fair to say that the answers have been there all along; we just do not allow them to come forward when we are trying to focus.

It is during non-focusing that the brain uses "**conceptual blending**" (the ability to make separate concepts and ideas co-exist), which is crucial to learning, performing and creativity. Instead of keeping all of our past experiences and ideas separate in our non-conscious mind, the brain will blend them together without our awareness.

The creative powers of the brain and mind amount to little more than the facility of compounding, transposing, augmenting, or diminishing information from our senses and experiences. The brain gathers dissimilar information from many different ideas to support what we are doing in the present. Breakthroughs often arrive when old ideas or past solutions are applied to new situations. Instead of keeping concepts separate, the brain – in all its wisdom – will unconsciously blend them together when we are not trying to focus.

Joydeep Bhattacharya, University of London psychologist, pointed out that interrupting focus brings forward the quiet, unconscious information in the back of our heads that helps learning, performing and creativity. While individuals were connected to EEG's monitoring brain activity, Bhattacharya and other researchers could recognize creative insights happening in the brain, before the individuals were consciously aware of them.

The corporate history of innovation at 3M labs is based on their scientists taking breaks from thinking about ideas for new products. Today Minnesota Mining and Manufacturing Company (3M), sells more than fifty-five thousand products, nearly one product for every employee. The first essential feature of 3M innovation is their "**flexible attention policy**," according to Larry Wendey, vice-president in charge of corporate research. Instead of insisting on constant concentration there is a 15% rule. Every researcher is allowed to spend 15% of their day daydreaming, allowing speculative insights to surface. The only requirement is that the researchers must share their ideas with their colleagues. This is much like how research shows that the brain blends different concepts together. The science of insights supports 3M's flexible attention policy.

Other interesting insights into how slowing down or discontinuing conscious focus enhances learning, performance and creativity comes from research by Beeman and Kounios. They saw a sharp drop in activity in the visual cortex when the brain was paying attention to its own prerecorded ideas and associations. (Everything about learning, performing and creativity is supported by associations – if this, then that.) Beeman pointed out that people often cover or close their eyes, slowing down the visual cortex, when thinking about solving a problem. When the outside world becomes filled with details the brain will automatically block them out. Messages with few or no distracting details are compatible with the nature of learning.

Studies by Beeman also demonstrated that people who score high on a standard measure of happiness test solve about 25% more insight puzzles than people who are upset or feeling angry. The relaxed feelings of delight can lead to dramatic increases in creativity and learning. Mental relaxation makes it easier to daydream and pay attention to subconscious insights. Jonathan Schooler, who helped pioneer the study of insights, said his lab studies have demonstrated that people who consistently engage in more daydreaming score significantly higher on measures of creativity. During a daydream the brain is blending together concepts that are filed away in different areas to form new connections that we call new insights. Without focusing the brain starts to explore its *inner* database, looking for connections in a relaxed fashion.

Scan tag to hear Michael speak about this
or Link to
http://youtu.be/8vTNQo2cIhE

NOTES:

_____

_____

_____

_____

_____

_____

_____

A Trick

One of the tricks for accomplishing meaningful learning is to find ways to nourish and enhance our personal imagination, thereby putting more life into growing new brain connections. It seems the prime mover for going from not knowing to knowing is the "skill of adaptation"– not fixing.

The music of mixing self-discovery; the environment; and self-evaluation is a sound track of imagination that can lead to meaningful long-term learning. This kind of music is the playful emotional component that is transporting approaches to learning on safe paths that are leading to the type of closure available from an unwritten contract between the brain and the kind of approaches to learning that promise to move students beyond just the hope of improving. Personal imagination can create images that are not available from how-to directions.

Personal imagination can joyfully touch the soul of the topic to be learned, setting off new connections in the brain as if the lights on Broadway were becoming brighter. Computer pioneer JC L Linklider said "85% of my time is spent getting into a position to think." Bring the brain – not just the body to leaning environments.

Today in the 21st century, there are many opportunities to be exposed to an overload of information before it can be changed into useful personal insights. By using modernized approaches to learning, information can become useable intelligence, thereby repairing the relationship between man and information.

Questioning if information has value and if the manner in which it is being shared is useful, are important questions.

It is estimated that 2.5 quadrillion bits of data are posted on the Internet every day. "But most of it is dumb data," said Peter Thill. In a *Wall Street Journal* article on 10 /20 /12 it was written that Peter Thill's choices of what to attempt to read and what not to read, were determined not by intellectual capability, but to a great extent by considerations of curious feasibility (his imagination).

It is important to note that by using approaches to deal with the information available, these approaches make important and useful adjustments that free up brain space for more intuitive and interpretive skills. We all can think, so let's allow our good brain to side-step poor approaches to learning and put to use all the personal conclusions encoded in our non-conscious minds that can support a variety of ways to reach workable outcomes.

The field of physics uses what is referred to as The Standard Model. It is given this name because it refers to standard common properties found in phenomena that can appear to have nothing to do with one another. Finding these common properties (a standard model) in different phenomena has provided insights into the causes of both wanted and unwanted outcomes.

The nature of learning also has what I would call a STANDARD MODEL. It is made up of elements that are found in all learning environments that support meaningful learning. These elements are fundamental to the nature of learning anything. This STANDARD MODEL provides insights into act of learning that when efficient they have the following common elements:

- An information delivery system
- Approaches that are free of negative criticisms and judgments
- Learning that is mostly not conscious
- Finds value in both wanted and unwanted outcomes
- Acts of learning take place in context
- Past experiences and prior knowledge support learning
- They are emotionally and physically safe
- They make students feel smart
- They use a playful approach to learning
- They realize outcomes are always inconsistent

The development of a positive transfer of information will embrace this STANDARD MODEL. It supports a process, not individual pieces of information. Paying attention to the *how* and the *why* of an approach to learning is more useful than placing the attention on details about a topic.

Failure to do so is questionable because of 21st century research into the brain's connection to learning. It appears that some traditional views about the topic of transferring information from provider to receiver can be almost like a religious commitment. But the pain of change is much smaller than the pain of regret. Process goals have been found to be more useful than outcome goals when learning. By embracing the process of learning and process goals, while avoiding focusing on the outcome goal of getting-it-right, meaningful learning is enhanced.

I ask, "Why can people be good at some things and not at others, and actually only really good a one or two things?" How was something accomplished when it was outstanding? What is being ignored, and what is being paid attention to in a simultaneous and sequential manor, allowing outstanding outcomes? Yes, what was being ignored can be more useful when learning than where the attention was focused.

Meaningful learning is a seamless process as all components come together on the same page, with the same goal of survival and meaningful learning, which are one in the same.

Metacognition

Writings about metacognition date back to the Greek philosopher Aristotle, if not further.

Metacognition is a mental skill that helps people perform cognitive and learning tasks. Both givers and receivers of information should develop metacognition skills. The term refers to the conscious and non-conscious mental activities involved in mental activities. It refers to mostly non-conscious, internal thinking involved in actively influencing learning in new situations. Examples include:

- Planning and approach to learning
- Monitoring comprehension of the activity
- Evaluating progress
- Distraction awareness - the ability to become aware of distracting stimuli both internal and external

Metacognition takes on many forms including insights about when and where to use a particular strategy for improving, seeing options, and problem solving. Efforts to enhance metacognition are arrived at by developing a learner's independence and their self-regulation skills. This is classified into three components:

1. Knowledge: What individuals know about themselves.
2. Regulation: Evaluating learning experiences through activities that help individuals influence their own learning.
3. Experiences: That have to do with current, on-going cognitive experiences.

Individuals with metacognitive skills are self-regulated learners who modify learning strategies and skills. They are aware of blocks to learning as early as possible and change tools and approaches to assure goal attainment. When tools and approaches are non-specific, general, generic, and content dependent, they are likely to be useful in different types of learning situations.

A brain-compatible approach to learning creates opportunities to learn from that are random (ever-changing environments), thereby enhancing metacognition skills. If we notice that we are having more trouble with learning "A" than "B", or when it strikes us we should double check "C" before accepting it as fact, are all examples of a capacity to regulate one's cognition to maximize one's own potential to think, learn, evaluate, and remember. Human beings do not come into the world with metacognitive skills. We come into the world with the capacity to non-consciously learn these skills.

Fixing is not learning, or investigating, or inventing. Fixing is acting on outcomes to understand, rather than on learning and the value of unconscious influences. To enjoy the process of learning is to enjoy hidden skills that value the acts of subtraction. Meaningful learning is more about *taking away poor insights*, than adding information.

Brain compatible approaches to learning are match-makers that blend new input with prior information stored in our non-conscious minds. Self-investigation can be a path to progress using enhancements that may seem counterintuitive, which is always a worthwhile investment.

The natural tools or natural system of coding and decoding information exists to inform self-examination, thereby revealing useful boundaries stored in the non-conscious mind.

Driving to a destination in a city for the first time without a GPS system can provide the advantage of getting a little lost and seeing parts of the area the GPS would have avoided. When walking around this city later you would have insights and information for finding your way around the area the GPS would not have exposed you to.

Teaching-fixing approaches are like GPS systems; the self-learning is being left out. On the other hand, learn and develop approaches know the value of getting a little lost and how that can develop future non-conscious reference points that support meaningful learning.

182

NOTES:

Part Six

Extra Credit

Reading this section is similar to extra credit work in a classroom setting. The following contains information that may only interest some readers, but it is information that can be used by every reader.

Short Notes from Harvard and Other Resources

- Change the way assignments of students are made is the first suggestion.
- Meaningful learning should not be a tricky business filled with frustration.
- The context and culture in which learning takes place will carry most of the responsibility for growth.
- Physical motions and emotions are influenced by words used, heard, read and by when they are used.
- When we discuss the nature of learning we are also talking about how emotions influence learning. Emotionally "safe" environments support long-term learning, while unsafe environments suppress growth and development.
- Identifying where students are is the best way to help them grow. When demand exceeds capacity – you fail.
- Individuals are either being, doing, or becoming, as they focus on the past, present, or future. Trying to become is not as useful as being and developing.
- Two components of memory are working memory and long-term memory. New information enters working memory for a very short time, normally just several seconds. This is where information is evaluated as not useful and set aside, or as useful and is sent on to long-term memory for future use.
- Working memory has a huge influence on learning. Information must make sense and have meaning for it to be sent on to long-term memory. Background information found in past experience can help working memory.
- Our working memory is trying to match patterns in new information with patterns in prior knowledge and past experiences. It is asking; does this information support survival? All learning is based on past experience.

- Stress, prior beliefs and some tasks can fragment working memory, which is operating in the same areas of the brain as attention. The brain recognizes patterns and sequences, not details. The brain is not concerned with accuracy – only what works for your survival.
- The brain uses small, general bits of information to make sense and gain meaning in the ever-changing environments the real world presents.
- The brain does not pay much attention to reputation – it cares about change and novelty.
- The brain makes things up to get by.
- The brain is fundamentally "goal oriented"– then moves on to a process goal.
- The brain uses internal networks for everything it does – it's a team effort – formed from similar and dissimilar experiences in different contexts.
- Skills and the brain are networks of cell connections, not a location. The biology of human development gives us insights into this ever changing reality.
- Learning causes networks in the brain to be rewired and to operate differently.
- The brain is always looking for patterns (not details), there by using as little energy as possible.
- Help individuals see old things in new ways.
- When they are learning help people calm down – there is no end to get – the journey never ends.
- Strategies – help grow intelligence – they are always individual, hopefully based on big concepts.
- Technology is only a tool, not the strategy that some have turned it into.
- Approaches to learning based on questions will last; approaches to learning based on data information do not last.

- We see the outcome of learning, not the process, or the many ways the brain can arrive at the answer.
- Observations are normally based on personal biases. Always look beyond behavior to find out the why of the how.
- Meanings get lost when too much energy is used to try and understand.
- People will always take away what their bias wants to take away. We don't mentally leave, we just ignore. We do or don't do, so we do not look bad.
- We will move away from facts when they are not aligned without personal beliefs. People make things up, or dump facts. Some just follow what they believe is the law – and do not see what really goes on.
- Comprehension and production of outcomes happen in different parts of the brain.
- Variables and inconsistency should be designed into approaches to learning, thereby converting sensations, sounds, and meanings into meaningful learning.
- There is a "zone of development" in which variability and inconsistency are opportunities, no one is broken.
- The aim is to improve the ability to take in information and evaluate words, perceptions, valuations and cognitivity in emotionally safe environments.
- The skill level of a performance is never at one point in time; it is always in a range of development. After reaching optimal level of performance, there will be regression to just a functional level then a return to optimal – inconsistency is a natural occurrence.
- A full range of conditions influence learning, there are always variations.
- Students are never in isolation.

- Looking inward will help focus attention on what we do outwardly. Recognizing and revisiting memories – reconstructing them, and then merging them with current experience.
- Skills are never completely "learned", they go up and down – there is progress and then regression where a lot of learning takes place.
- Suggestion: change the way assessments are done!
- Help individuals invent their own skills.
- The nature of learning is always tinkering, an instinct that is useful during problem solving.
- A patchwork of past personal wanted and unwanted outcomes, unconsciously led by our curiosity, supports meaningful learning.
- Human beings are meant to be a participant, a doer, who is in charge of the relationship with their environmental experiences.
- Antonio Demasio, (neurobiologist of the mind who heads Univ. of Southern California's Brain and Creativity Institute) stated, "Our brain processes stimulus (information) before our consciousness is aware that we have perceived it. A process that takes place effortlessly and without awareness."[51]
- Fact: The brain thinks consciously about one thing at a time. Any other decisions are made automatically by our unconscious mind.
- Joseph LeDoux, (New York University, author of *The Emotional Brain*), stated, "Most cognitive processes haven been found to occur unconsciously, with only the end-product reaching the conscious mind – if at all. Contrary to

---

[51] The Feeling of What Happens, by Antonio Demasio, p. 121

popular belief, the conscious process involves an unconscious processing mechanism." (p. 67)

- Lorna Rale, Ph.D, (Head of Department of Neurobiology and Behavior at Columbia University) states, "Non-conscious brain power, most of the time, is moving along and working on things of which we are totally unaware of."

- See consciousness like a TV screen and the unconscious mind like the wiring inside the TV. Conscious mind can handle 50 bits of information, while our unconscious mind holds thousands of bits.

- Einstein once said, "Not everything that can be counted counts and not everything that counts can be counted." Some things are learnable, but not teachable.

- Learning is often less about subject matter information and more about human nature, interest, and will.

- When looking at the history of human evolution we are also observing the history of the nature of learning. This view reveals how, over time, human beings and human brains simultaneously grew up together, guided by nature and nurture. The development of human intelligence and acts of meaningful learning were both a predisposed natural process (a survival skill). There is a need to constantly keep things new and fresh to experience meaningful learning.

- As the teacher I often start by saying, "give me a lesson." Learning what students already know is a valuable starting point.

- Predicting a wanted outcome starts the process. Help students develop the tools of acquisition – help them become aware of the environment. We change on the inside first, and then change on the outside.

- Physical instructors include books, teachers, etc. Non-physical instructors include memory, fear, imagination, emotions, curiosity, etc. and they are more important.

- Make the mind, body and emotions a seamless team – the food of intellectual growth is a variety of activities, in different contexts, that come together.
- Natural and spontaneous activities are effective ways of experiencing learning, giving learning a quality of personal freedom and engagement.
- Dr. Wall, "Human development depends on the success with which the fundamental emotional needs of individuals are being met". The function of approaches to education is to provide the best possible emotional conditions for growth and development.
- Growth is something that an organism does for itself. No one can grow for another, or learn for another. **Growth is from within, but it can be stopped by others.** Educators should be guided by the general concerns of the student. Education is an atmosphere, a culture and largely unconscious.
- The natural law of growth demands the fulfillment of each stage of development for its own sake, not for some other end product.
- The aim of education must be to inspire and keep curiosity alive. Learning is waves of self-discovery. It is possible to get good grades, be first in class and miss the purpose of education.
- At times the error or weakness of education is to be preoccupied with information to the exclusion of any other aspects of learning.
- The efficiency of learning is directly in proportion to the extent to which individuals are wholly bound up in learning from outcomes, while not trying to get something right or fix anything.
- Education and learning are conceived and born from personal insights and "ah - ha!" moments.

- By trusting from the very start that the interactions of the body and mind spontaneously work together, meaningful learning arrives.
- The most valuable teacher is in the soul of the student. There is no mental development, without emotional safety. Learning must be for self in all of us.
- Meaningful education is not only supplying information, but acts on individuals so they become their own best teacher. Look for practical takeaways for students, avoid technical details, the brain does not need them.
- Follow the natural laws of development and individuals gradually transform into their own self-reliant educator.
- Meaningful education helps individuals learn to think, to find out, to have "ah - ha!" moments, to invent.
- The great essential factor in education is to make individuals feel secure, safe and smart as students.
- Self-expression, without the pressure of trying to get something right or please others, goes a long way when learning.
- A meaningful approach to learning promotes the freedom for individuals to be themselves and learn in their own best way.
- Meaningful learning arrives mostly not by what students are told, but by what they find out for themselves and through practical use make their own. Learn from the whole of the experience and not merely from books and lectures.
- Meaningful learning approaches stretch students just beyond their present abilities. Such approaches students seek out activities that they are not that good at.
- U.S. Olympic Committee psychologist stated, "No matter what the topic is you want to take students out of their comfort zone, but in a safe environment".
- Change the context of the problems each time. There is a need for approaches to learning to develop students with

flexible and portable skills, which can adjust to unforeseen challenges.

- Cultures and customs create an environment, and wire the brain to work in that environment. Change the customs and insights of a culture, to change outcomes.
- The right approaches to learning create brain activity; this brain activity leads to outcomes. Some approaches to learning release chemicals that suppress learning and others release the kind of chemicals that support learning. Brain chemicals include: Dopamine, Cortisol, Oxytocin, Vasopressin, Serotonin, and Norepinephrine.
- Skills are a network of cooperating connections formed in the brain. These networks are formed from experience, context, and perceptions during the biology of human development. The <u>brain</u> uses networks for everything we do.
- The nature of human development could be referred to as the nature of learning. Human beings did not evolve to fail, but 50 species a day become extinct on earth – and we are still here.
- The brain sees and uses patterns and sequences in the world to make patterns within the brain for future reference.
- We do not unlearn, we learn to ignore.
- Learning strategies are tools that promote gradual development, not perfection.
- There is a "culture" of development in which inconsistency is an opportunity. Have flexible approaches, no one is broken in need of fixing.
- The level of a performance is never at one skill level – it is always in a range.
- Meaningful learning involves revisiting memories, reconstructing them, and then joining them with current experiences.
- Skills are not built linearly – they go up and down

With the Brain in

Mind

"The future of learning lies in the study of the brain."
Dr. Donald Thomas

Toolbox

The mind-brain could be seen as a mental toolbox, one that is very different from any toolbox we may have at home. The toolbox at home is filled with tools that are designed for specific operations; to hammer, to saw, to twist on and off, to screw in or out, etc. These kinds of tools can break and wear out. On the other hand, the mind-brain is filled with equipment that is always developing. The mind-brain can develop to the point where it has flexible knowledge and portable skills that can accomplish the variety of interactions required for living in ever-changing real world environments.

After birth (and before birth) our interaction with the environment causes the mind-brain to develop its equipment. These interactions cause new connections to grow between the cells (or neurons) in the brain. We could say that the original tools that the healthy brain comes into the world with are constantly learning and (being modified), becoming more flexible and portable. On the other hand, the toolbox in our home contains tools that can wear out.

See these connections (wiring) between the cells in the brain as highways that are always (24/7) carrying the information inside cells to other cells. These connections are like little tree branches reaching out to connect with each other. This large network of connections gives human beings a very efficient information highway (toolbox) or survival tool for learning. "Our brain contains a kind of mental tool box developed over millions of years of evolution to help our ancestors survive and reproduce in challenging environments."[52]

"Everyone can learn to learn," said Ronald Gross of Peak Learning. To improve acts of learning, provide individuals with the

---

[52] *Mind Wide Open*, p.9

tools to adapt and experience meaningful learning. Let's see learning as the ability to transform facts into usable know-how knowledge.

"I love to learn, but hate to be taught."
Winston Churchill

When you try to change an unwanted outcome you can win or lose, but when you help the individuals learn you always win. Keep in mind; trying to teach is different from helping someone to learn.

In the February 2010 issue of *Education Leadership,* Daniel T. Willingham, a cognitive scientist from the University of Virginia stated, "Ignoring research based on the principles of learning can have negative effects on student learning." Non-compliance with how the brain decodes, encodes and recalls information can create roadblocks and detours away from meaningful learning.

Anthropologist Richard Leakey states, "The past is the key to the future." Our first non-human ancestors appeared on earth about a billion years after what is referred to as the Big Bang. Human beings belong to the species Homo sapiens, which means "smart being." The learning qualities of the human brain and mind have been shaped by an evolutionary journey starting with the earliest living non-human organisms (our ancestors) billions of years ago. This insight supports the view that the human brain has always been wired for survival from day one. Studies show that fifty species a day become extinct on earth and over ninety percent of the species that once lived on earth no longer exist, but human beings still do!

Connections

Human intelligence grows when the number of connections between cells in our brain are increased by interacting with our environment. How the brain grows new connections is influenced by the design and structure of the environment where the development takes place. These connections exchange information between cells throughout the brain. This chemical or cell sharing of information about our environment has supported the survival of the human race from day one.

Unlike a camera that captures only one frame at a time, the brain's cellular networks operate like a large committee making millions of decisions simultaneously. I gained this insight while attending Harvard's Mind-Body Connection to Education classes.

The brain does not have a notebook or blackboard where information is recorded. Information in the brain comes in the form of neurotransmitters that travel between the cells in the brain (chemical-electrical back to chemical messages). This chemical, electrical process is influenced (positively or negatively) by the approach to learning that is being used. Reasoning, decision-making, and learning are all chemical in their origin and this connection should not be overlooked if approaches to learning are expected to be efficient.

When the approach to learning is brain-compatible every human being is capable of encoding information that can be recalled by a healthy brain. An act of meaningful learning is a natural instinct, a gift or benefit of evolution. New learning has always been, and will always be, an active process based on all of life's past experiences.

Learn-and-develop approaches to improving should not be seen as a ladder that is rising straight up to a state of knowing. The process of learning and developing is always creating new connections in an existing web of many connections scattered throughout the brain. In the 21st century many in the education community have started to realize that having some understanding of the brain's connection to learning can open new pathways and can enhance natural learning skills.

Positive-Assessment Form of Learning[53]

The authors of this paper said, "We have argued that an absence of an investment in the understanding and refining of **positive-assessment practices** is a notable oversight in the field of sports. This significance is both a moral obligation, as well as a valuable condition for ensuring that any assessment decisions are learning oriented."

Coaching practices and outcomes can be enhanced through the establishment of **positive-assessment practices** that are learning oriented. The engagement of the athlete in the collection, interpretation, and implications of acts of positive assessment can enhance outcomes when learning.

Purposeful positive-assessment involves students planning to collect performance evidence for informing ongoing learning and performance when development (not fixing) is the aim.

Feedback, in itself, may not promote learning unless students are positively engaged with it (Gibbs, Simpson). The use of teaching aids provides too much support, thereby suppressing learning (UCLA Learning Lab). Armour points out in his book *The Learning Coach*, that regardless of the demand on the sports coach, positive-assessment learning is central to quality coaching, even at the high end of the professional performance spectrum.

Learning and pedagogy concepts have traditionally been outside the domain of sports coaching. However more contemporary research has demonstrated that "coaching is really about learning" [54] "Pedagogy" relates primarily to the interactions between the coach and player. On the other hand, a *"learning-message"* refers

---

[53] Source: published research from the *School of Human Movement Studies,* University of Queens Land, St. Lucia Australia.
[54] *Sports Coaching Cultures; From Practice to Theory,* by Jones, Armour, Potrac, p. 21

to the information (explicit and implicit) necessary for performing, including rules, tactics and skills needed.

Although learning and pedagogy have been recognized as foundational to the practice of sports coaching, the current use and value of positive-assessment components of coaching **are notably absent**. Researchers now believe that this is a significant oversight. Failing to recognize this key aspect of learning and pedagogy overlooks opportunities for optimizing the development of both the coaches and athletes.

When positive, the assessment approach can promote the learning of:

Targeted knowledge
Process
Skills

Positive assessments support having students assess and apply the necessary what-to-**do** knowledge during learning for themselves, not what to fix.

The components of efficient positive assessment include:
Learning-orientation

Learning-Oriented assessments provide positive what-to-do information that is accessible and interpretable by learners and instructors alike.

Authentic

Authentic assessment is concerned with the relationship between learning content and the context of the assessment used. Assessments must be positive and meaningful to the learner and **relevant to the context** in which the knowledge and skills will be used. This involves a demonstration of knowledge and skills in the mode in which they will be engaged in a performance context.

Validity

198

Validity, this measurement must satisfy six conditions –
content, substance, structural, generalizable, external and
consequential elements. In other words what needs to be
valid is the information collected the means of its collection, the interpretation and the positive implications and
consequences for learning.

Social

Socially, all learners/performers are given equal opportunities to engage in positive assessment. This includes the importance of providing multiple (a variety) opportunities to
demonstrate evidence of performance in ever-changing environments, ensuring that learners are engaging positive assessment in a context that suggests learning. Learning-oriented positive assessments help people learn to engage in
the process and become familiar   with the standards they
are going after. **In these environments the person learns
to better understand (and appreciate) their own
strength and areas that further their development.**

The term "feed forward" was coined by D. Bond to indicate
the notion of using positive-assessment feedback to assist in the
improvement of future performances and allows athletes to become
assessors of their own learning. Through this positive process of
self-reflection, athletes learn to access, interpret and use positive
feedback about *what to do* (not what to fix) in order to improve future performances.

The Unconscious Brain and the Athlete[55]

Athletes are known for their physical skills, but unconscious
brain activity also has a vital role in optimal sports performance.
John Milton states, "Brawn plays a part, but there is a whole lot

[55] Source: A paper by research scientists John Milton- Claremont College; Sian Bellock- University of Chicago; Daniel Wolpert- University of Cambridge; Emanuel Todorov- University of Washington.

more to it than that. The body depends on the brain for non-conscious directions."

When athletes think consciously about mechanics a pool cue, a golf club, or a tennis racquet can start to feel like a foreign and unwieldy instrument. Athletes, who have less noise going on in their sensory input and motor output systems, will have the edge when it comes to learning and performing. **The brain is a very active organ with duties that go way beyond just guiding a motion, making it difficult to consciously focus on a particular event**. Efficient brain function is energy cost-conscious, using as little energy as possible when operating, thereby relying heavily on unconscious input.

After a workable outcome athletes often struggle to explain exactly what they did. Sean Bellock states, "They do not know what they did specifically, so they do not know what to say." They just did it. The brain has the ability to unconsciously anticipate actions in advance and update responses as needed. Research has uncovered that the brain goes into action before we move. Some research studies state this occurs a few seconds in advance of movement. This is an *unconscious* process.

Milton said he and his colleagues used MPI scans to monitor blood flow in the brain and found that devoting conscious attention to swing mechanics could actually hurt performance, even among professionals.

Research suggests that when professional golfers think too much about their shots, they activate parts of the brain that they have not used in golf since they first learned motions. Studies show this throws the brain's ability to use our automatic motor pathways out of whack. Milton continues, "This happens because the advanced athlete has developed motor pathways to figure out solutions and conscious thinking will disrupt existing brain patterns."

Gabriel Wolf, a scientist from University of Los Vegas, author of *Attention and Motor Skill Learning,* points out that the automatic motor pathways that process the brain are fully capable of engaging motions that will shut down when athletes think about how to move their bodies. (This is a brilliant insight that has enhanced my approach to instruction.)

The experience of "Being in the Zone" could simply be what happens when the brain regions that make athletes conscious of their movements are quiet; leaving the motor centers free to unconsciously guide the player to victory. The ability to perform without consciously thinking is called "automaticity", giving athletes an advantage!

Ideally, during the heat of the game (or when learning), athletes should process sensory data they are taking in and then automatically deliver a motor response, without conscious thought. They should just do it!

In his book, *On Intelligence*, Jeff Hawkins points out that the brain is a "prediction making organ," which is a survival skill. The brain uses internal representations, so it can predict what may happen next. This process is called, "forward modeling." This model allows athletes to pre-plan "what they want to accomplish and how they are going to accomplish it" (non-consciously).[56] The brain's unconscious forward modeling skills determine the best way to move, reducing delays in body movements. Forward models provide reference data from previous experiences that are essential for crafting motion. Both wanted and unwanted past outcomes are valuable influences for forward models.

Forward models are referred to as "priors", and are not set in stone. This is a good thing, since rarely are environments or scenarios in sports (or life) exactly the same. The accumulated information from all past experiences, (priors, wanted and unwanted), allow athletes to react favorably to the unexpected. The inconsistencies of outcomes are a natural variable that support growth, development and learning. (Golf is not hard, it's inconsistent.)

The brain's predictive skills are constantly being updated with new or different sensory information as it executes a motion.

---

[56] Emanuel Todorov, University of Washington

This is a natural feedback loop (survival skill) that helps the body to maintain influence over movements. "Given your goal, given where you currently are (developmentally and context), the feedback loop puts forward (unconsciously) the best way to get there."[57]

The way the nervous system interacts with our motor system isn't flawless. At times there is "noise", or sensory static that prevents our muscles from learning or using the message the brain is sending. This noise comes from conscious thinking, leaving the athlete with a distorted image of the state of their game. Studies show players with less noise gumming up their sensory-motor systems are predisposed to athletic success. With fewer disruptions these players are able to engage strong, fast muscle contractions that are incredibly accurate.

Self-doubt and concerns will slow down learning and skill development. Sian Bellock says, "In stressful situations, athletes become worried about the consequences of the situation and their thoughts disrupt their ability to allocate attention (unconsciously) to where they need to be," (which is – just do it!).

Malfunction in the prefrontal cortex (the center of the brain's reasoning, emotional and focusing abilities), is primarily to blame. **Bellock pointed out that stress prompts the brain to try to control information that should be left outside of conscious awareness, causing what she refers to as "paralysis by analysis."**

Deep versus Wide

Wide and deep learning are different. Wide learning involves knowing a wide range of information about a topic. Deep learning involves knowing a lot about a small range of topic information. Deep learning allows athletes to apply what they know to

---

[57] Todorov

situations in different or new contexts. Deep versus wide learning was researched by a "Who's-Who" team of scientists from the National Science Research Institute at the University of Chicago American. The use of "transfer skills are the Holy Grail in the whole thing."[58] **The transfer of skills from one discipline to another is a result of deep learning.**

Sian Bellock: "Often, athletes can tell you exactly what they are doing when they screw up. It's a misallocation of resources. Worry and the brain becomes too busy. The motor cortex, which controls the planning and execution of movement, should be doing most of the work unconsciously. On the other hand, athletes often cannot tell you what was happening when winning. They have no conscious memory."

When athletes start thinking about details of their techniques instead of just letting their unconscious run the show, they tend to mess up. In the University of Chicago's Human Performance Lab, players who were asked to focus on details, which engaged their performance cortex, made more errors than players given no instruction.

Similarly, while teaching at Arizona State University, Dr. Robert Gray, now a senior lecturer in motor control at University of Birmingham in England, asked baseball players to identify if their bat was moving up or down at certain moments. Their swings suffered. Jocks should be dumb and not think about much, using working memory rather than unconscious motor pathways."[59] Where is the start of that quote?

In many people's eyes, doing things *by the book* would be the best approach to learning. Unless the book is based on insights that are personal in nature, doing things by the book will probably not facilitate long-term learning. Fortunately, there is a fictitious book authored by three billion years of evolution and natural selection entitled *Nature's Plan for Learning.*

---

[58] James Pellegrino, co-director LSRI.
[59] Time Magazine, article by San Gregory; July 30th, 2012 issue

Nature's plan connects the mind-brain to learning and it contains all of mankind's predisposed urges and instincts that evolution passed on to guide man in the direction of learning and surviving. With nature's plan, each individual is mentored to create their own plan which is: **do, observe,** and if needed **adjust** based on past experiences.

The components of meaningful learning include: emotional, social, cognitive, physicals and reflective components.

All five components function simultaneously. No component can be completely turned off. Each component's action affects all the others, as part of the whole. Every question or problem can touch all component.

- **Emotional** = Safe, personal insights and interests
- **Social** = Collaborate, self-evaluation, authentic, personal decision making
- **Cognitive** = Reasoning and deduction skills based on past experiences
- **Physical** = Active hands and minds learning, not passively following
- **Reflective** = Makes all other components efficient with non-conscious record of past experience

In order to be encoded, long-term information must connect with all these components seamlessly. For example: information must touch emotions and interest; be challenging; be personally relevant; connect with past knowledge and also be independently complete. Emotions must be safe as personal interest leads to fun and challenges create growth.

An efficient mind-brain-compatible approach to learning is a process that engages and coordinates an individual's ability to construct the appropriate neural cell assemblies of self-discovery while simultaneously self-assessing their interactions with the environment. It all happens at the same time.

Any implications and limitations of insights, questions and answers about anything (including acts of learning), depend on the story we choose to tell ourselves. It is useful to create those stories about learning with an open mind.

"To improve, most approaches to education would have to stop doing almost everything they do in the name of improvement."[60]

Because emotions are a critical component of meaningful learning, how individuals see themselves when learning often has to change. Stanford University Ph.D Carol S. Dweck refers to how we see ourselves as a "Mindset," the title of her must read book.

For example, when learning, some individuals see themselves as, "I have something missing," or "I have things that need to be fixed." On the other hand, individuals who see themselves as who they are at that moment are in place to start a journey of new learning and developing. They do not see themselves as broken, in need of fixing or having something missing. That no one is broken, in need of fixing or missing something is an important mindset for both the givers and receivers of information in any learning environment.

The motion we first make or the knowledge we currently have should be seen as who we are. Then in the future we can learn to use first motions, or current information base, in different ways. When learning, our prescriptions, balance, rhythm and timing should be seen as developing and not in need of being fixed.

The nature of learning is the nature of human development, a process that is fueled by an engine that is doing more than just gathering subject content information. It is an engine that is fueled mostly by how individuals see themselves when they are learning, which is heavily influenced by the design and structure of the

---

[60] Collins, 2001, p.91

approach for learning that is being used by the providers and receivers of information.

After meaningful learning has been encoded and we are accomplishing a different outcome, we have not fixed anything; we are learning to use the perceptions, balance, rhythm, and timing that we started with differently. Fixing isn't learning.

Flexible Knowledge – Portable Skills

"How does the mind work and especially how does it learn?" is the question asked by Daniel T. Wellingham, of the University of Virginia, Neuroscience – Cognitive Psychology Department, at the beginning of his article, *Inflexible Knowledge.*

The following was compiled from and influenced by this article published in the winter 2002 issue of *The American Educator*.

What are the steps and stages of learning? First, mankind's brain has a bias for remembering new concepts and information in terms that are superficial and concrete, not in terms that are abstract and deep. But individuals who have mastered skills have flexible knowledge, (not superficial) and portable skills, (not concrete).

Experts, (if that's what they should be called) can *transport* what they are learning in one environment, (knowledge and skills) to dissimilar conditions and contexts. Unfortunately, in some approaches to education people are not gaining the insights and training that allows them to transport what they are learning beyond their current conditions. These individuals are learning what science calls, "inflexible knowledge and non-portable skills," and are just being conditioned.

In learning environments that are supported by **self-development through self-discovery,** knowledge becomes flexible and skills become portable. Approaches to learning that do not give learners the opportunity to use their own curiosity, imagination, and their "what if I did this" ideas, tend to develop information that stays concrete and superficial not deep. It is the approach to learning that can determine whether or not information becomes flexible or inflexible knowledge.

The aim of a good education is to enable students to apply new concepts and new information to situations that go beyond classrooms, practice fields, labs, or golf practice ranges. For example: a yang child with flexible knowledge who wants to paint a narrow line, but is holding a three-inch wide brush, will turn the three inch paint brush on its side and use the narrow side to achieve his desired results. On the other hand, a child without flexible knowledge will look for a thinner paintbrush. While this is a simplistic example, it demonstrates the difference between flexible and inflexible knowledge, (self-development through self-discovery develops the kind of portable skills and flexible knowledge that following directions does not).

Professor Daniel T. Wellingham, "The human mind appears to be biased towards learning the surface features of problems and at first is not concerned with grasping the deep structures that are necessary for achieving flexible knowledge and portable skills." This may be why traditional approaches to instruction that are founded on "here's my money, tell me what you want me to do," are both popular and educationally vacant at the same time. A reason there is a large volume of how-to instruction available, (that is always changing) is that our mind has a bias towards the features of problems. **Workable approaches to learning move people beyond this bias into flexible knowledge and portable skills.**

"Memorizing with an absence of meaning," would be an informal definition of rote learning, (which is the bogeyman of education) Professor D.T. Willingham, "We would like students to gain insights and meanings. A good education seeks to develop creative problem solvers, not parrots. In so far as we can, we must prevent students from absorbing information in rote form." (Using drills and copying expert models are examples of rote learning found in math, history, grammar, sports, etc.).

Some approaches to instruction are conditioning students with rote learning techniques. There is a difference between learning and conditioning. When we are encoding and learning we are not just gathering rote information without insights and meanings. **Conditioned students have narrow, inflexible knowledge, lacking any deep structure that is portable.** For example, many golfers who lack flexible knowledge and portable skills overlook the fact that the principles for applying and aligning force in the putting motion are the same principles that are used for the motion of a longer swing. Eighty-five percent of the driver swing's application of force can be transferred from an efficient putting motion. A self-discovery approach to learning gives people the opportunity to become their own best teachers by enhancing their ability to respond to ever-changing environments as they expand and construct flexible knowledge and portable skills.

Webster defines learning as, "acquiring knowledge by experience," and education as "training by which people learn to develop and use their own mental and physical skills." The joy of learning and a good education often does not come from teachers; it can be based on nature's plan for self-development through self-discovery. Traditional approaches to instruction can limit possibilities. On the other hand, nature's plans for efficient learning evoke unlimited support for the arrival of new insights.

Traditional instruction is often over-dressed with steps that do not create a healthy link between a learner and his environment. Traditional instruction can be like standing on a slippery slope and trying to get to an exact point, instead of being fascinated by the journey. **In learn-and-develop environments students are softly courting all the possibilities; they are not looking hard for the *answer.***

Be a private investigator and report to yourself what you notice about your environment. Become your own reporter, not a follower, who looks for someone else's impressions. Good coaching, mentoring, or guiding will help people notice what is being overlooked. Everything we notice has meaning and input for future reference. Everything has application depending on your point of view. What your brain is encoding is either workable or unworkable, and both are valuable for learning. Knowing the left and knowing the right helps to identify the center. There is no failure, only accurate feedback in workable learning environments.

Interest Before Fun

Keeping students interested by giving them choices and allowing them to use their own curiosity and imagination, births meaningful learning. In the view of research from the science of learning, it is interest that brings on the fun of learning. When students are not making progress, but what they are learning still holds their interest, fun and progress can follow.

The human brain is a sense-making organ that is drawn in the direction of what interests its natural curiosity. It is after students are interested in solving the problem, that the fun involved in learning follows. Sports psychologist Dr. Rick Jensen has pointed to the value of training techniques that keep students interested and curious.

Some learning environments are not the engines of change and mobility they could be when personal insights get lost in someone else's corrections. But by linking up what the science of learning is uncovering about approaches to education, the joy of learning anything, even golf, can be experienced.

Effective managers in the business community and effective educators build confidence in the power of curiosity, imagination and what-if ideas of others. They help individuals find insights that are personal in nature for the problem to be solved. Allowing the illusion of how-to directions from a perceived expert to take over a learning environment only slows down gaining knowledge that is personal in nature for future use. We all come into this world curious to learn with an urge to invent survival skills and develop our own information base. To have the mind energized by an interest and the urge to keep looking may be more valuable than a positive outcome. The energy of anticipating what's next can be more powerful than the satisfaction of completing a task.

Praise and Learning

Those who maximize their potential as educators, coaches, employers, or parents interact with people in ways that cause individuals to trust in their own inner abilities as they are growing and developing. Having the self-confidence that what we are learning to do will have a positive outcome is imperative.

Dr. Haim Ginott stated in his book Between Parent Child, "Praise without judging; anger without hurting; acknowledging someone's feeling, perceptions, and opinions, rather than arguing about them; criticizing without demeaning; discipline without humiliating; are the tools of individuals who gain the trust of their students, players, employees, and children." **Having accurate information to share is not enough; the skills of sharing and helping people learn are also required.**

Ginott went on to say, "In psychotherapy, judgmental and evaluative praise is avoided. You are great; you are a good student, are not used. Why? Because it's not helpful. It creates anxiety, invites dependency and evokes defensiveness. These statements are not conducive to growing self-reliance, self-direction, and self-control, all qualities that demand freedom from outside judgment. Self qualities require reliance on our inner motivation and inner evaluation." **Students, players, employees and our children all need to be free from the pressure of evaluation praise with others becoming their source of approval.**

Goal: to rephrase Dr. Ginott; praise consists of two parts; what we say to individuals, and what in turn individuals say to themselves. Our words must state clearly what we like and appreciate about someone's effort, work, help, consideration, creation or accomplishments. Our words must be ones on which people can build a positive picture of themselves. It will take some thought to be *"specific and descriptive"* in our praise, but those who hear them will benefit from this kind of appreciation and information much more than when they are evaluated and judged through praise. For example: "The bookcase you built looks beautiful," is helpful praise that can create the positive inference, "I am capable." Less helpful praise would be, "I think you did a great job."

"Your composition gave me several new ideas," is helpful praise giving the positive inference, "I can be original." Less helpful praise, "You write well for your grade. Of course you still have a lot to learn."

"That's the type of golf swing that can work anywhere on the course" is helpful praise. "That was a great swing" is less helpful.

"You handled the problems with that new account just right," is helpful praise. "You are a great salesman" is not.

Using descriptive statements that create positive conclusions in the mind of individuals become the building blocks of emotional health, an important element of anyone's ability to experience meaningful learning

Praise was compiled from notes I made while reading, *Between Parent and Child*, a must read for valuable insights into learning.

Yin and Yang

We could say the nature of learning has a yin and a yang. The yin is: it seems that nature's plan for the human race is for mankind to evolve, survive, succeed, and not fail. The yang: because we are all designed to succeed, we have the ability to learn without consciously trying to learn. **Biologically it's not possible to learn anything directly.** Sound research shows that learning is grounded in parallel processing and past experiences or indirect preparation.

What causes learning? What is the origin of learning? Perhaps we could say the origin of efficient learning is a human being's basic will to survive. This will to survive enhances the "self" found in self-discovery, self-development, self-assessment, self-confidence, self-etc. How human beings operate is also influenced by chemicals produced by our bodies and brain. When discussing the origin of learning the chemicals produced by our system could be seen as partners with, and at the core of, acts of learning – the Yin and Yang.

Are you ready to learn? The mind-brain is always ready to learn – but this readiness can be fragmented, moving individuals off task in teach-to-fix and get-it-right environments.
The computer industry is presently focusing on the optimization of search engines and critical thinking appears to be the brains' search engine. Critical thinking (seeing options) that's spontaneous, improvisational, and creative, often uncovers what we were not previously aware of; these skills are at the heart of thinking

Attention – when we are not paying attention in a meeting – all past meetings we have been in become less valuable. Attention is normally associated with the present, but it is our past experiences, when we are paying attention, that provides the most valuable insights.

In the Beginning

When discussing human development, insights about learning are more easily uncovered (in my view), by starting from the beginning. The term "uncovered" is accurate for describing what is being discussed here. The nature of learning has existed we could say, from the beginning and it waits to be uncovered and recognized for its value by everyone who is not happy with his or her progress.

Over time, nature has predisposed elements of our *being* with natural instincts and urges to interact with the environment. These seldom talked about urges and instincts are preparing us for learning. These urges and instincts are designed to open full fields of interest, as learners become explorers making their own choices and adjustments. It is with efficient preparation that learning takes hold.

It may help to see this preparation as having two stages. One stage occurred during evolution and natural selection. The other stage of preparation is driven by man's urges and instincts that encourage people to be curious and develop a variety of different insights that can prepare them for learning anything. Before man can emulate, he must be prepared.

Nature's plan for learning is not concerned with perceived perfection in models. For example, once a child or adult is launched on their attempts (by their urges and instincts) to learn, they will often improve on any examples set for them. A learner's instincts are designed to drive him to do something, to do anything definite. In the *doing*, people are learning about organizing, interacting, and staying on task.

People enhance the steps and stages of learning every time they do something definite, (not perfect), and one day they can advance beyond any examples that inspired them to use their urges and instincts.

The urges and instincts to do something definite should not be corrected, they should be observed. The outcome of the to-do instincts is feedback, (never failure) for future reference. People develop and organize their preparation skills for future learning through what could be viewed as indirect preparation. The choice to-do something definite becomes indirect preparation for learning anything. Learning is learning and everything we learn is indirect preparation for learning something else.

Before we can learn, we must be prepared to do so. This preparation for the most part is indirect preparation, having little to do with new learning. Preparation is a skill that is derived from man's natural urges and tendencies *to-do*. Expert models are there to inspire and motivate man to make an attempt, they are not there as a blueprint to be copied. **Nature is not concerned with a perceived perfect model; one that is just in-the-ballpark will do just fine**. In fact, once launched on his attempts to learn, man often improves on any model he may have had. It's during this stage of learning that nature is giving man an opportunity to develop his or her decision-making skills, or said another way, improve his preparation for learning.

When a child, (a learner) decides to do something definite (void of possible physical harm), even if it seems absurd to us, he should to be allowed to finish. If this curious to-do cycle of activity is interrupted, the results can be a loss of interest. The science of learning has uncovered that it is highly important to let these cycles of to-do action run their course. **The brain, through indirect preparation, is training itself for direct learning.** Any type of interaction with our environment is preparation for other types of interactions we may want to have in the future, even when these interactions give the appearance of having no reasonable connections. **Direct learning, if we call it that, is based on indirect preparation.**

The paths of efficient education follow the path of evolution. The instinct to-do, or to experience the indirect preparation of passing through one discovery to another, is part of nature's evolution and nature's plan for learning. The idea of exploration or scouting should become an element of any approach to education. **It is not a good thing to split life into living and learning.** Robert Sapalsky, Ph.D, Stanford University, points out that memory from indirect preparation, leads to learning, which leads to behavior modification.

Tinkering

Research teams at the University of Washington's Institute for Learning and Brain Science are collaborating with Stanford University on a five year project that links neuroscience and education. I would call these research projects acts of tinkering in a wonderland of what may be learned.

Acts of tinkering are often not seen for their value, or even put to use while wondering what an outcome may be. This lack of tinkering can cause gaps in learning, and little growth in deduction and reasoning skills.

Learning to tinker and wonder more deeply supports innovation, collaborating and problem solving, thereby enhancing bottom line results.

Unfortunately, there is often an over-reliance on best practices from perceived experts and approaches that cannot accommodate rapidly changing environments. On the other hand, personal tinkering skills (wondering) can address problems that were not anticipated.

It is not possible to create standardized plans to address ever-changing conditions. But decisions based on tinkering with past experiences and domain knowledge are useful in all environments.

Sully Sullenberger, who landed a commercial plane filled with passengers, safely in New York's East River said, "One way to look at this landing might be for 42 years I had been making small regular deposits in my brain's memory bank made up of all my past flight experiences. Then, on Jan 15, 2010, the balance was such that I could make a large withdrawal of information to help me land the plane safely."

We do not need a neuroscientist to tell us that our brain is calling the shots, but we may need one to learn about how this internal brain process influences how we go from not knowing to knowing. Poor or misinformed interpretations of the nature of learning that lack the power of tinkering in wonderland can become the unfortunate foundation of inaccurate theories for approaches to learning.

Intelligence

In 1994, fifty-two respected scholars formulated a scientific consensus and defined intelligence as "the ability to reason, plan, solve problems, think abstractly, comprehend complex ideas, learn quickly, and learn from experience; the ability to catch-on, make sense of things, and figure out what to do."

Our brain is not a notebook where information is written; it is a malleable, living organ that can intuitively assemble proper brain connections. Efficient approaches to learning draw individuals into acts of playful curiosity about their own questions. Efficient approaches to learning do not ask us to merely follow directions, which may not fully engage the higher cortex of our brain where learning happens.

Indirect Preparation and Direct Learning

One of the most important discoveries from research is that learning *always* takes place against a backdrop of existing knowledge. Past experiences are a form of indirect preparation for new learning. The term "transfer of learning" makes reference to how new learning connects with past experiences, allowing new information to be transferred more efficiently to long-term memory. When we are encoding new information, depending on one's past experiences, it is either useful or not. **Past experiences reveal our options, not the answer.**

Research has shown that individuals from all age groups can indirectly enhance their ability to learn while they are in school, attending seminars, doing workshops, or in any other learning environment, through what they experience (similar and dissimilar) beyond formal education settings. In other words, what you learn in one setting can greatly help you in other settings. Nature wired mankind to learn by *doing*, *observing* outcomes, and then if needed, *adjusting* as we see fit, based on the indirect preparation of all of our past experiences.

This stage of learning is called parallel possessing, as what is going on in the present is paralleled to or cross-referenced with the patterns, sequences, perceptions and classifications that are formed from what we have already experienced. Again, when performing or learning a particular activity or taking in new information, these acts are guided by the indirect preparation gained from the memory of all of our past experiences (workable, unworkable, and similar and dissimilar) that is encoded in our subconscious.

Before we learn we must be prepared. This preparation is for the most part indirect, having little to do with what is to be learned in the present. Preparation is a skill that is derived from our natural urges and tendencies *to do*. Studies have demonstrated that experts are there to inspire and motivate us to make an attempt; they are not there as a blueprint to be copied.

Nature is not concerned with a perceived perfect model; one that is just-in-the-ballpark will do just fine. In fact, once launched on his attempts to learn, man often improves on any model he may have. It is during this stage of learning that nature is giving us an opportunity to develop our decision-making skills, or said another way, improve our preparation for learning.

When a child (a learner) decides to do something definite (without possible physical harm), even if it seems absurd to us, he should to be allowed to finish. This is a duplicate sentence if this to-do cycle of activity is interrupted, the results can be a loss of interest. The science of learning has uncovered that it is highly important to let these cycles of to-do action run their course. **The brain, through indirect preparation, is training itself for new learning.** *Any* type of interaction with our environment is preparation for other types of interactions we may want to have in the future, even when these interactions give the appearance of having no reasonable connections. **New learning is clearly based on the indirect preparation gained from all our past experiences.**

Meaningful learning follows a path of evolution. The instinct *to-do* receives support from the indirect preparation that our past experiences provide, connecting one discovery to another, which is nature's plan for learning.

In nature's plan for learning, the first attempts are attempts that form the skills of preparing for new learning. This subtle insight is not so subtle when it comes to having accurate insights about the nature and joys of learning. Learning is the end result of indirect preparation or what has been previously encoded in man's brain and mind.
The influences of indirect preparation on direct learning cannot be undervalued.

The idea of exploration, or scouting, should become an element of any approach to education. **It is not a good thing to split**

life into living and learning. Robert Sapalsky, Ph.D, Stanford University, points out that memory from indirect preparation leads to new learning, which leads to behavior modification.

It is a poor concept to feel that when a model or example is copied it would help students learn to do likewise.

Meaningful learning is based on experiencing all the stages (the ups and downs) of preparation. This is nature's indirect approach and preparation for learning. Indirect preparation has a wide range of outcomes, some workable, others unworkable, some similar, some dissimilar that develops flexible knowledge and portable skills. This is one of the most important elements of long-term progress – an insight is often overlooked and undervalued.

#1 The culture of teach-to-fix **approaches to learning is now considered outdated and could be seen as an example of a human being's gift for attacking itself, causing individuals to lower their self-image.**

#2 One of the aims of this book is to support every individual's unique way of making progress by focusing more on the nature of learning, than just on subject matter information. Improving one's ability to learn is influenced less by accurate facts than by the culture and customs of the environment that individuals are being asked to learn in.

Our Brain, What a Gift!

Meaningful learning and gaining a good education are influenced by expectations.

- What expectations should individuals have when learning?
- What expectations should individuals have about the learning environment they are in?
- What knowledge and skills are needed to be an efficient learner?

- Should a good education accomplish knowing the answers to test questions? Or…does gaining a good education accomplish the development of life-long learning skills for use beyond classrooms?

Theodore Sizer said, "Estimating, imagining, and reasoning are at the core of learning. What meaningful learning should accomplish lies in how different the following two statements are when it comes to the brain based emotion of expectation."

First, there is the classic statement that elected officials, educators, and at times parents often use; *every child in America has the right to receive a good education."* Pause for a moment and consider what expectations this statement creates about learning?

This second statement is an edited version of the first; *"every child in America has the right to have the **opportunity and support to earn a good education."*** What expectations does this statement create about learning?

The term *receive* a good education creates a very different tone, mind-set, and expectations than the term *earn* a good education. The view here is that meaningful learning and a good education are ***earned***; that lessons are *acquired*, not given.

In the October 2008 issue of *The Advocate*, a National Education Association publication stated, "The one that does the work does the learning; life-long learners have learned to learn on their own; they have developed the ability to evaluate themselves; they take control of their own learning; they develop metacognitive skills". Metacognition is defined as "cognition about cognition", or "self-knowing about knowing."

There are many important insights about brain-compatible approaches for earning a good education that are not being put to use at a speed equal to their value. But how can any approach for *earning a good education* and experiencing meaningful learning expect to reach its potential without first taking into consideration the nature of learning and the biology of human behavior?

Brain-compatible information delivery systems always put forward information with the brain in mind. These approaches help the brain to stay engaged when making predictions, the most useful tool for earning a good education.

On the other hand, the higher cortex of the brain may not fully engage the deduction and reasoning skills of a self-reliant, life-long learner when the expectations are that it is the responsibility of the learning environment is to give individuals a good education. When the expectations are that individuals are going to follow directions and *receive,* rather than *earn and gain* a good education, it is an approach that is not as brain-compatible for meaningful learning.

Unfortunately, the world is filled with a vicious cycle of messages of instant success, quick fixes and fast temporary relief, all leading us away from meaningful learning. It is small, short steps and long plateaus between steps that support meaningful learning.

We all possess unused potential. It is our evolutionary destiny to keep learning throughout our lifetime. Always cultivate the mind and heart of a beginner rather than getting ahead of yourself. Be willing to spend time on the plateaus of development engaged with the process of learning and not focusing on the end product. It seems as soon as you ask, "how long will it take," you are also looking for results, which can slow down meaningful learning.

A better way to enjoy learning is to avoid the pressure of authoritative (how-to) treatments of learning, thereby dismissing the emotional problems that can exist in get-it-right approaches to improving.

The Guestimating Mind

Thanks to the brain's intuitive grasp of probabilities (guestimating), it can handle imperfect information. "Instead of trying to come up with an answer to a question, the brain tries to come up with a probability that a particular answer is correct," said Alexander Puget of the University of Rochester and the University of Geneva in Switzerland. In his book – *On Intelligence,* Jeff Hawkins also notes how the brain operates by making predictions.

Studies into the value of probability-based thinking and learning are largely based on the work of Thomas Bayers, an 18th century English clergyman. He proposed that a claim is more reliable if that belief included an assessment, or some initial belief known as "priors."

These "priors" can be updated as more information comes in, narrowing the range of good solutions. At the heart of this concept is the notion that when learning from experiences, both workable and unwanted outcomes lead to better predictions and probabilities.

In a way, it is self-evident that humans rely on existing knowledge. A brain that did not rely on its experiences would be operating below its potential. "You could argue that it would be a little strange if we were bad at predictions," stated Geisler, University of Texas at Austin. About predictions Geisler says, "It's something that we have enormous experience with, evolutionarily."

Geyser and his colleagues have found humans "almost perfect" at predictions founded on past experiences.

Sixteen-month-old children can make correct assumptions, if this, then that, when faced with complicated data. This was reported by cognitive scientist Laura Schultz and Hyawon Gwen.

In the past learning may have been about what some believe to be great content, now it can be about *enhancing approaches to learning*. It has been found that non-compliance with how the brain decodes, encodes and recalls information can create unfortunate road blocks and detours away from meaningful learning. Gaps in knowledge about meaningful approaches to learning have caused many disappointing and frustrating learning experiences for both givers and receivers of information. Fortunately, these gaps have been getting smaller since the 1990s. For over the past three decades modern science has been uncovering some keys for enhancing approaches to learning.

NOTES:

_____

_____

_____

_____

_____

_____

_____

_____

_____

_____

_____

_____

_____

_____

_____

_____

_____

_____

_____

_____

Short Thoughts

&

Acronyms

Short Thoughts

- Information that is geared for helping you is not as valuable as information that is geared for helping you help yourself.

- How can any approach to learning expect to be efficient without first taking the nature of learning into consideration?

- Meaningful learning is mostly a predisposed natural non-conscious process that is first engaged automatically in a mother's womb before we are born.

- Brain-compatible approaches to learning develop the skills to develop more skills.

- Brain-compatible approaches to learning use 'play,' (acting in a way that seems OK) while learning is developing, rather than acting in accordance with an exact plan.

- Brain-compatible approaches to learning focus on changing a student's insights and perceptions, not on fixing unwanted outcomes.

- Brain-compatible approaches to learning enhance learning potential.

- New learning is based on past experiences.

- In brain-compatible learning environments there is no failure, only usable feedback for future reference.

- Brain-compatible approaches to learning offer students choices.

- Acts of efficient learning are made with the best ingredients on earth; curiosity, imagination, and improvisation.

- Efficient approaches to education see students as lights that are burning bright and these approaches are geared towards helping students help themselves to burn even brighter.

- Trying to teach is different from helping someone to learn.

- Telling has never been teaching and listening has never been learning.
- Mankind is designed for success, not for failure. We are all competent self-learners and efficient self-teachers. We self-learn first, and then simultaneously self-teach to use what we have learned for surviving and thriving.
- The main focus of educators, instructors, parents, or employees should be to make individuals with whom they are sharing information feel smart and self-reliant.
- Encourage the joy of doing, instead of trying to out-do!
- The individual who creates the poor outcome is the one who should determine what to do to create acceptable outcomes.
- What is it from the past that is getting in the way of future progress?
- Do not be in such a hurry to get a situation under control that the lesson to be learned gets overlooked.
- Going to school or taking a lesson is one thing, becoming educated is another.
- Following directions or restating facts when learning does not engage personal evaluations, synthesis, reasoning or deduction skills, stifles motivation and diminishes creativity, turning the joy of learning into drudgery, with a negative influence on self-image.
- Learning is influenced by change and unfortunately many individuals believe making a change requires trying to get something right, or trying to fix something. Studies show that fixing has never been learning and trying to get-it-right creates the kind of stress that fragments progress.
- What we do not know can hurt us, but if what we believe is not true, or is incorrectly interpreted, it also hurts us because it fragments progress.

- The brain is a sense-making, problem-solving ever changing dynamic organ. The emotional mind may like calm, but the critical thinking, looking for options brain uses chaos.
- If students are not learning and changing, then approaches to education have to change.
- Minds are like parachutes; they work best when they are open. Many minds have become air balloons, and we know what they are full of!
- Ordinary things can produce extraordinary results. Note: the numbers 1 and zero are running every computer in the world.
- Strive for excellence with what you have and what you have will improve.
- Students accomplish what may seem impossible when teachers see it as possible.
- Workable learning environments are not looking for perfection; they are guiding the skills of performance improvements.
- Efficient approaches to learning ask students what they would like to improve.
- Efficient approaches to learning improve a student's capacity to learn; i.e. learning potential.
- Students want to learn; judge them and they <u>will not</u> make the kind of progress they could.
- Create self-motivation. Develop a trusting nonjudgmental environment.
- After learning potential improves, performance potential improves.
- Students often reveal the best way to help them experience the kind of learning that lasts.
- Learning is brain-on, hands-on, entertainment, as students invent their own skills.
- Pointing out poor outcomes is a poor motivator.

- It is important to ignore poor outcomes and redirect behavior elsewhere.
- How effectively individuals learn depends on where educators put their focus. The more attention paid to any behavior (poor or good), the more that behavior will be repeated.
- Students must trust their teacher and trust grows and develops when teachers provide non-judgmental environments.
- Trust grows by focusing on the positive with a proactive approach.
- Create trust with the principle of do no harm.
- Teachers always reinforce something and it is what teachers reinforce that grows.

Play with Word Acronyms

- **GAPS** = **G**one **A**re **P**ossible **S**olutions
- **AWARENESS** = **A**lways **W**elcomes **A**rriving **R**ealities, **E**valuating **N**ew **E**nvironmental **S**ights and **S**ounds
- **LEARNING** = **L**ong **E**verlasting **A**wareness, **R**eveals **N**ew **I**nsights **N**urturing **G**ains
- **LEARN** = **L**ive **E**xperiences, **A**ctivate **R**eliable **N**urturing
- **TRY** = **T**alking and **R**idiculing **Y**ourself
- **GOLF** = **G**aining **O**ngoing **L**asting **F**un
- **FAILURE** = **F**inds **A**ccess **I**nto **L**earning **U**ncovering **R**eal **E**xperiences
- **DNA** = **D**elivering **N**atural **A**ctions
- **CELL** = **C**an **E**xpress **L**earned **L**essons
- **PLAY** = **P**owerful **L**earning **A**bout **Y**ourself
- **SMART** = **S**tudent's **M**inds **A**re **R**eally **T**alented
- **SAFE** = **S**tudents **A**lways **F**irst **E**nvironment
- **GAP** = **G**uides **A**ctual **P**erformance
- **MIND** = **M**any **I**nternal **N**ever-ending **D**ecisions

- **BRAINS** = **B**ring **A**ttention **I**nto **N**ew **S**ensations
- **LIFE IS** = **L**everaging **I**nsights **F**rom **E**xperiences **I**nforming **S**uccess
- **HUMANS** = **H**ave **U**nconscious **M**inds **A**lways **N**avigating **S**ituations
- **EDUCATION** = **E**ngages **D**eductions **U**nder **C**onditions **A**ctivating **T**houghts **I**nvolving **O**utcomes **N**oticed
- **FRUSTRATION** = **F**inding **R**easons **U**nconsciously **S**tealing **T**rue **R**easoning **A**way **T**hrough **I**nvolving **O**ngoing **N**egativity
- **IMATATION** = **I**nvolves **M**any **A**ssumptions **T**hat **I**nterpret **O**utcomes **N**ow
- **GAME** = **G**iving **A**nyone **M**ore **E**njoyment

To Be Continued…

"We never know what the future holds,
especially when it comes to what may
be possible.
I know I will keep looking –
best of luck pursuing your goals."
Michael

Bibliography of
The Short Story Based on Book Titles

The Power of Their Ideas, By Deborah Meier

The Engine of Reason, The Seat of The Soul: A Philosophical Journey into The Brain, By Paul Churchland

From Neurons to Neighborhoods:
By Committee on Integrating the Science of Early Childhood Development, Youth and Families Board on Children

Mind Wide Open, By Steven Johnson

The Playful Brain, By M.D. Richard Restak & Scott Kim

Between Parent and Child, By Dr. Haim Ginott

Between Teacher and Child, By Dr. Haim Ginott

Brain-Friendly Strategies for the Inclusion Classroom, By Judy Willis

Activating the Desire to Learn, By Robert Sullo

Habits of the Mind, By Archibald Hart

Places for Learning, Places for Joy, By Theodore Sizer

Theory of Instruction: Principles and Applications, By Siegfried Engelmann

Fantasy and Feeling in Education, By Richard Jones

The Naked Brain, By Richard Restak

The Everyday Genius, By Peter Kline

The Power of Play: Learning What Comes Naturally, By David Elkin

Peak Learning, By Ronald Gross

The Talent Code, By Daniel Calle

The Art of Awareness: How Observation Can Transform Your Teaching, By Deb Curtis

A Mind of Its Own, By Cordelia Fine

The Emotional Brain, By Joseph LeDoux

Bright Air, Brilliant Fire: On the Matter of the Mind, By Gerald Edelman

Origins of Intelligence in Children, By Jean Piaget

The Science Behind What Makes Us Unique, By Michael Gazzaniga

What Does It Mean To Be Well Educated?, By Alfie Kohn

Science, the Brain and Our Future, By W.R. Klemm

Bibliography

- *Smart Moves* — Dr. Carla Hannford
- *Mindstorms* — Seymour Papert
- *Mindfulness* — Dr. Ellen Langer
- *The Power of Mindful Learning* — Dr. Ellen Langer
- *Mastery* — George Leonord
- *How the Mind Works* — Steven Pinker
- *Cooperative Learning* — Dana L. Grisham / Paul M. Molinell
- *Becoming an Effective Teacher* — Amy Seely Flint
- *How to Think Like DaVinci* — Michael J. Gelb
- *Seven Steps to Genius* — Michael J. Gelb
- *The Seven Dimensions of Intelligence* — Dr. Paul E. Dennison
- *How People Learn* — National Research Council
- *The Absorbent Mind* — Maria Montessori
- *Magical Child* — Joseph Chilton Pearce
- *Chewing Gum and Walking* — Yocum
- *Peak Performance: Mental Training Greatest Athletes* — Charles Garfield
- *Reframing* — Richard Bandler
- *Heart of the Mind* — Connirae Andreas
- *Run Your Brain For a Change* — Bandler and Andreas
- *The Power of Now* — Eckhart Tolle
- *Working With Emotional Intelligence* — Daniel Goleman
- *Talks to Teachers* — William James
- *The Art of Being* — Erich Fromm
- *Emotional Intelligence* — Daniel Goleman
- *Working Knowledge* — Thomas R. Bailey / Katherine l. Hughes / David Thornton Moore

- *The Owner's Manual For the Brain* — Pierce J Howard, Ph.D
- *The Quality School Teacher* — William Glasser, MD
- *A Brain for All Seasons* — William H. Calvin
- *Synaptic Self (How the Brain Becomes Who we Are)* — Joseph LeDoux
- *A Brief History of the Mind* — William H. Calvin
- *The Book of Life* — Stephen Jay Gould
- *Cognitive Neuroscience (The Biology of the Mind)* — Michael S. Gazzaniga, Richard B. Ivry, George R. Mangun
- *Seeing with The Mind's Eye* — Mike Samuels M.D., Nancy Samuels
- *The Human Mind Explained* — Susan A. Greenfield
- *Inside The Brain* — Ronald Kotulak
- *Discover Your Genius* — Michael J. Gelb
- *The Birth of Your Mind* — Gary Marcus
- *Between Parent and Child* — Dr. Haim G. Ginott
- *Teacher and Child* — Dr. Haim G. Ginott
- *The Society of The Mind* — Marvin Minsky
- *Mindsets* — Carol S. Dweck Ph.D
- *The Mind* — John Taylor
- *On Intelligence* — Jeff Hawkins
- *Teaching for Understanding* — Martha Editoi Stone Wisk
- *Out of Our Minds* — Ken Robinson
- *The Naked Brain* — Richard Restak, MD
- *Bounce* — Matthew Syed
- *Helping Students Learn in a Learner Centered Environment* — Terry Doyle
- *The Brain that Changes Itself* — Norman Doidge, MD
- *Don't Believe Everything You Think* — Thomas Kida
- *Teach Like a Champion* — Doug Lemov
- *The Secret Life of Two Grown* — Barbara Strauch

Up Brain

- *Horace's School* — Theodore R. Sizer
- *A Place for Learning, a Place for Joy* — Theodore R. Sizer
- *Toward A Theory of Instruction* — Theodore R. Sizer
- *Learning to Teach, Teaching to Learn* — C. Doug Bryan
- *Spark* — John A. Ratey MD
- *A Mind of its Own* — Cordelia Fine
- *Mind Hacks* — Tom Stafford
  Matt Webb
- *Brain Rules* — John Medina
- *Peak Learning* — Ronald Gross
- *The Playful Brain* — Sergio Pellis
  Vivien Pellis
- *Bright Air, Brilliant Fire* — Gerald Edelman
- *Everyday Genius* — Gary Alan Fine
- *The Emotional Brain* — Joseph LeDoux
- *Origins Reconsidered* — Richard Leakey
  Roger Lewis
- *The Seven Sins of Memory* — Daniel Schacter
- *Multiple Intelligence* — Howard Gardner
- *Creativity, Flow* — Mihalyi Csikszentmihalyi
- *An Introduction to Piaget* — R.G. Richmond
- *Higher Order Thinking Skills* — R. Bruce Williams
- *The Learning Leader* — Douglas B. Reeves
- *A Mind at a Time* — Mel Levine
- *Global Brain* — Howard Bloom
- *Making a Good Brain Great* — Daniel G. Amen MD
- *Talk to Teachers* — William James
- *The Tree of Knowledge* — Humberto, R. Maturana, Ph.D
  Francisco J.Varela, Ph.D
- *Learning Through Movement* — Betty Rucke
- *Welcome to Your Brain* — Sandra Aamodt, Ph.D
  Sam Wang, Ph.D
- *The Well Educated Mind* — Susan Wise Bauer

236

- *Human Development*   **Kurt Fischer**
- *Ten Steps to Complex Learning*   **Paul Kirschner**

Jeroen J. G. van Merrienboer

CPSIA information can be obtained at www.ICGtesting.com
Printed in the USA
LVOW08*1442080913

351500LV00014B/54/P

9 781937 069056